39.95

MANAGERIAL ENGINEERING

MANAGERIAL ENGINEERING

Techniques for Improving Quality and
Productivity in the Workplace

RYUJI FUKUDA

Foreword by Norman Bodek
President, Productivity, Inc.

PRODUCTIVITY PRESS
Cambridge, Massachusetts

To help you utilize the information in this book, Productivity, Inc. has developed a training course in conjunction with Dr. Fukuda to teach the totality of Japanese management practices and principles in quality and productivity. If you are interested, please contact Productivity, Inc., 750 Summer Street, Stamford, Connecticut 06905 or phone (203) 967-3500

Originally published by the Japanese Standards Association in 1982 as:

企業活力を生みだす
管理技術開発のすすめ
—QC, IE, OR の実践的活用法—

Library of Congress Catalog Card No. 83-62993
ISBN 0-915299-09-7

Productivity Press
P.O. Box 3007
Cambridge, MA 02140
(617) 497-5146

Excerpts from *Loud and Clear: The Full Answer to Aviation's Vital Question: Are Jets Really Safe?* by Robert J. Serling. Copyright © 1969 by Robert J. Serling. Reprinted by permission of Doubleday & Company, Inc.

Printed in the United States of America
First English edition   6

Typeset in Novarese.

CONTENTS

FIGURES

TABLES

TABLES

FOR

FOREWORD

I first met Ryuji Fukuda in March 1981 while I was leading my first industrial study mission to Japan. During this two week tour we met with managers from sixteen of Japan's leading corporations. Our group of nineteen American senior executives was really fired up about discovering the secrets of Japanese management. What truly lay behind the "miracle" of Japan's quality and productivity gains? What was kanban? How effective, really, were quality control circles, and how did they fit in with the management culture? Above all, *were the techniques being used here transportable to American soil*, or were they specific to the society of Japan?

We spent about half a day at each company we visited. During this time we had very little opportunity to get to know our hosts. They tried to be helpful, but for most of the trip, it was difficult to overcome the barriers of language and culture in such a short time.

The one exception was Ryuji Fukuda, at that time a senior executive with Sumitomo Electric Industries Ltd.

He did much more than go through the formalities; he obviously wanted very much to teach us. He wanted us to understand that even though we spoke a different language, even though we looked different to each other, human nature was the same all over the world, and that if we could really see this, then we would be able to bring the lessons of Japanese management back with us to the United States.

Ryuji had tremendous barrier to overcome. He didn't know us personally. He couldn't speak English, and at that time he had very little translated material we could read about his work.

However, I was aware that he had won the Deming literature prize. I felt like a diamond prospector who discovers a fortune, but only sees before his eyes the cloudy stones. Something inside me told me that the diamond was there and that somehow I was required to do the polishing.

I found out that Ryuji could read English, and started to correspond with him. Then I invited him to speak at my next "Productivity the American Way" conference, which was to be held in New York City November, 1981.

By November, Ryuji was working with Meidensha Electric Manufacturing Co. Ltd., a subsidiary of Sumitomo. The president of Meidensha had asked the president of Sumitomo for help on quality. He specifically asked for Ryuji, who was appointed to the board of directors and put in charge of quality in all their production facilities.

Ryuji came to New York, where his presentation was very well received, and I began to understand the full power behind his work. As he said to me then: "I am not teaching quality control; I am teaching foolproof methods for reducing and eliminating defects."

It was at this time that I made a commitment to translate his work into English and help him teach his concepts to American managers.

CEDAC® is the process that earned Ryuji the Deming prize. Like many of the other methods he teaches in this book, there is a magic in CEDAC. It is the magic of utter simplicity. Most of what you will read you already know, but have never been able to put into practice. As I did on my initial journey to Japan, you must go deeply into the teaching. You will find the words easy to read and understand, but you must work very hard with the author. You can do that by making a point of looking for ways to apply the principles to your own work.

In this book you will really learn how to apply your own knowledge. Ryuji is teaching you how to mobilize all of your experience as a manager and develop for yourself a clear path to managerial success.

There is no mystery to Japanese management. Most of the basic principles were discovered in the United States many years ago. Ryuji has only looked at them and put them to work scientifically.

I have read this book many times, and each reading leads me to new discoveries. I wish the same for all of Ryuji Fukuda's American readers.

NORMAN BODEK
Publisher
Productivity, Inc.

ACKNOWLEDGEMENTS

The English verson of *Managerial Engineering* is realized by the courtesy of the Japanese Standards Association, an organization for promoting industrial standardization, which is under the control of the Agency of Industrial Science and Technology, Ministry of International Trade and Industry of Japan (MITI).

The author is grateful for the assistance and support provided by Sumitomo Electric Industries Ltd. and Meidensha Electric Manufacturing Co. Ltd.

The publisher wishes to acknowledge the assistance of the following people: Noriko Hosoyamada, translator; David Perlstein, editor; Russ Funkhouser, book cover designer; Marie Kascus, indexer; and Patricia Slote, production manager.

INTRODUCTION

Foreigners share a widespread misunderstanding that everything runs quite smoothly in Japanese plants. This misunderstanding must be corrected. In fact, much time and effort were needed to achieve the present success of Japan's leading companies. For example, worker group activities, which have become famous worldwide, did not work at all fifteen years ago. Even now, as many as one-third of the major Japanese manufacturers cannot benefit from employee participation.

It is important for us to supply unbiased information on Japanese plant management. I fear that foreigners may otherwise take Japanese methods as a mysterious formula for quality and productivity. They may mistakenly conclude that Japan is a mysterious land where any problem is solved magically. Such misunderstanding obscures the actual efforts of Japanese engineers and workers which should be of interest to foreign firms. The mistaken notion that Japan is a peculiar, mysterious and completely different nation from others does not provide the basis for true friendship and cooperation, but rather, danger of international conflict. It is not difficult to avoid such misunderstanding; telling the simple truth will suffice.

To apply the principles of Japanese plant management in overseas plants with different social and cultural environments, we have to analyze our approach to management in terms of two categories, namely, that which is inherited from traditional Japanese culture and values, and that which is universally applicable. If the former factors predominate, the application of Japanese plant management in a foreign country will be impossible. If, on the other hand, the latter factors dominate, Japanese management methods can be helpful, if not wholly applicable.

I am convinced that the basic methods of quality control, industrial engineering and operations research are applicable in all plants, Japanese and non-Japanese alike.

In November 1981, I was invited to a three-day conference in New York sponsored by Productivity, Inc. With the theme "Productivity – The American Way," the conference brought together about forty speakers and 400 participants, for the most part American. They came from various business organizations, schools, government, and even the Army and Navy.

As the only foreign speaker, I presented my ideas on managerial engineering with actual case studies from our study group approach to CEDAC,® OET, IE improvement and day-to-day management.

I concluded my presentation with the statement that if I were an American manager, I would do my work by taking into account three conditions and one difference (which follow) and thus secure high quality and productivity in my operations.

Many missions are sent from the United States and other countries to study Japanese management. Our company, Meidensha Electric Manufacturing Co. Ltd., welcomes more and more of them every year. Books and reports concerning

Japanese management are published one after another.

It is often said that unique characteristics of Japanese firms, such as lifetime employment, employee loyalty, the promotion system, democratic decision-making, intra-company unions, etc, are the causes of successful management. But if this were true, all Japanese firms would show high efficiency and profitability.

In fact, there are many Japanese firms with these characteristics which are also poor performers. Therefore, we must compare not only Japanese and foreign firms, but also successful and unsuccessful Japanese firms. The latter comparison will provide truly valuable information for those who want to learn from successful Japanese management.

From my experience, I maintain that the managerial engineering techniques presented in this book would have been impossible without the following conditions:

(1) Top management's support for managerial engineering;
(2) The understanding and cooperation of labor unions;
(3) Employee interest and satisfaction in creative activities.

As for the first condition, most of Japan's top managers have long recognized the critical role of high product quality as a source of competitive advantage, and expressed this need in their management policies and leadership. They developed company-wide quality goals and quality improvement programs, and made significant efforts to implement them. Quite a few Japanese firms require their divisions to report quality control activities to top management. At the same time, huge investments were made for large-scale, company-wide QC education programs. It was this long-term QC education that spread concepts and methods of quality control in Japanese firms.

Top management's support is also observed in other

fields. At Meidensha Electric, both the president and chairman attended the employees' study circle for personal computers. Through this experience, all the employees learned what top management was aiming for.

The strong support from top management spreads down through every management level. The "don't speak" rule for OET activity, discussed in Chapter 6.1, would have been impossible without the plant manager's support. If the plant manager had refused to support this activity, foremen would have felt obliged to speak out to show off. And if the plant manager had not allowed them to spend as many as 190 man-hours a month for meetings, the plant would not have been able to reduce the defect rate by 90%.

During my presentation, I asked what American managers do to encourage managerial engineering and what investments they make for long-term results. It is true that Japanese firms do possess favorable characteristics that facilitate plant management, but these are not sufficient conditions for success. Actual efforts, such as those made by top management, are much more important.

Incidentally, Japanese plant management is often described overseas very selectively. One hears of employees singing the company song and doing exercises every morning, and even the manager's knowledge of the traditional Noh dance that helps him make managerial decisions. Even the Japanese people are unable to explain how these factors encourage high quality and productivity. This kind of misinformation is often brought to foreigners by the Japanese themselves. They will kindly explain what foreigners wish to hear about Fujiyama and shogun. I regret that this kindness brings only misunderstanding and even suspicion on the Japanese.

To return to the subject, the second condition concerns the cooperation of unions who work with management to achieve high performance goals. The first goal of the union is to promote the employees' welfare and interests, but it can also contribute to the prosperity of the corporation, which in turn leads to employee satisfaction.

Mr. Donald F. Ephlin, vice president of the UAW, gave the keynote address at the New York conference. He affirmed the union's willingness to cooperate with the auto companies as long as this is for reasonable goals. It would appear that this second condition is becoming a reality in the United States.

The third condition expects workers to work not only for money (which is the principle motivation in any country, of course), but also for the pleasure and satisfaction obtained through creative activities such as improving operations.

It seems to me that these three conditions now exist in the United States. Emphasizing these three conditions, it is my goal to provide the reader with correct, unbiased information on Japanese management that will help them understand their own situation.

Now, there is an important difference between Japan and the United States. I once heard an anecdote: a group of Japanese tourists was traveling in the United States. They ordered a rental bus at a hotel. The next day they got on the bus and waited for the driver, who never showed up. The hotel manager explained to them that they had ordered a bus, but not a driver. They should have ordered both. This is an interesting story which illustrates a fundamental difference between our two countries. "Doing only what is ordered" is interpreted as a criticism in Japan. But what if the hotel manager above had been a computer, not a human being? The person who input a vague instruction would be at fault, not the dull-witted computer.

English has an expression, "butting in," which means interfering in someone else's job or activity. In countries other than Japan, this kind of butting in is strictly prohibited by custom, and the work system is designed so as to clearly delimit each worker's area of responsibility.

This is the main difference between Japan and other countries. When a worker group provides ideas for an improvement project, they are butting in on what is traditionally the responsibility of engineering. But it is possible to develop a work system where constructive interference of this sort is not only accepted, but expected to contribute significantly to higher performance.

If worker group activities are to be used in participative management schemes in the U.S., this sort of behavior will have to be encouraged. Since many American companies are now developing QC circles, I would think that they have started dealing with this problem. I sincerely hope that American firms obtain the three conditions, overcome the difference, and thus succeed in the development of new, American managerial engineering.

On the other hand, Japanese managers must learn the American way of work in the age of automation.

Computers cannot work in the Japanese system of reaching out beyond one's limited area of personal responsibility. Under Japanese management, the worker is constantly expected to reach beyond the strict limits of his job.

It is imperative for American management to start thinking along these lines. The Japanese, on the other hand, will have to learn how to restrain this type of behavior. Automation is only one reason for this. The other is that the younger generation in Japan is becoming increasingly westernized. It is obvious that in this world of international communication, Japan will not be able to maintain its unique values and traditions forever, as the law of increasing entropy suggests.

As American management approaches Japanese techniques, the latter must approach the former from the opposite direction. Once they are implemented, reliable methods and practice are a permanent source of wealth for the

Free Information!

If you liked this book, you may be interested in some of our other publications on Just-In-Time, Japanese management, productivity and quality improvement. Just drop this card in the mail and we'll put you on our mailing list.

Company Name _____

Address _____

City/State/Zip _____

Name _____

Title _____

Phone _____

TITLE of book I found this card in _____

This book was a ☐ purchase ☐ gift

PRODUCTIVITY, INC. P.O. Box 9102, Cambridge, MA 02140-9922 (617) 497-5146

manufacturing firm, but the situation in which this wealth is used is subject to changes in the external environment. The firm must predict future changes and take appropriate action. Both American and Japanese firms will find, according to their characteristics and decisions, some appropriate balance between American and Japanese management.

It is important for Japanese firms to explore ways of developing QC circles in the United States. This will not only pay off for American firms, but for Japanese companies ten years down the road.

When I had finished this presentation, many participants came up to shake my hand. At that time I was impressed by the great strength of the American people: the will and ability to think frankly and try to improve themselves. The audience evaluations of my presentation, sent to me by Norman Bodek, president of Productivity, Inc., were very high. In fact, their evaluations expressed more their impression of Japanese management than the quality of my presentation. It was truly encouraging to see that the ideas and approaches to managerial engineering which I have explained in this book were so well received by these representatives of American management. Furthermore, the conference provided the opportunity to publish the English-language version of this book.

I wish much success to all managers as they set out to improve productivity and quality, and hope this book will prove useful to them in that quest.

RYUJI FUKUDA

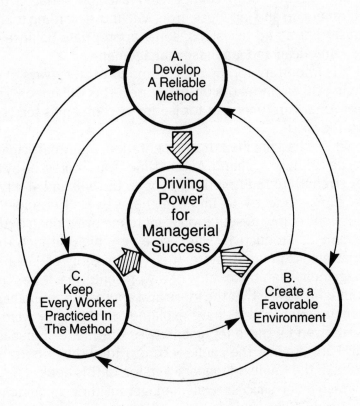

Figure 1-1 Driving Power for Management Activities

Chapter 1

PRINCIPLES OF MANAGERIAL ENGINEERING

1.1 THE SEARCH FOR A RELIABLE METHOD

Is there a management method which can always reduce manufacturing defects by 50% or yield a fixed rate of productivity growth whenever it is used? "Too good to be true," the reader may be thinking.

I think that managerial engineering techniques such as QC (Quality Control), IE (Industrial Engineering), and OR (Operations Research) all originated in the demand for a *reliable method*. An expert working alone will achieve very little with management techniques such as QC and IE. Working together, however, a group of people can use these techniques to secure significant results. My past experiences — including both success and failure — have convinced me that when we as a group work towards the completion of a new project, we can only push forward if we possess a reliable method. No matter how often we talk to workers about improving product quality, words alone will do nothing to promote real results. On the contrary, we need to find a system, a method, which leads us inevitably to success when its procedures are followed step by step. As managers, we all want to obtain such a useful tool. I emphasize the word "tool." In fact, I went through much study

1

and research before concluding that managerial engineering is a tool.

About two decades ago, Sumitomo Electric Industries Ltd. won the Deming prize.[1] Prior to this event, the company had started an initial QC study program. At the time, I was a member of the Production Engineering Department. As was usually the case with young engineers in the factory, I was overloaded with work. Then, out of the clear blue sky, headquarters created the new task of Quality Control. When I look back on those days, I cannot help but feel embarrassed. I actually thought my new QC responsibilities were unrelated to my daily work. I was completely unaware that QC was a useful tool. Consequently, I felt that my work had doubled because of this new job. Aside from my urgent everyday tasks, now I had QC to contend with.

Each department received lectures on QC from visiting professors. As beginners, we took this new technique as the golden rule. Therefore, when we were unable to understand or apply this new knowledge, we tended to blame ourselves for not studying hard enough. As a result, we dove into ever more sophisticated QC techniques.

In 1975 I was assigned to the head office as IE department manager, responsible for managerial engineering, which covered QC, IE and OR. My goal was to help my staff and workers avoid the mistakes I had made in the past. Over the years I had developed my philosophy of managerial engineering: it is a tool that can be applied by anyone to solve the problems of even the most troubled section of a company.

To meet these requirements, a useful method had to be developed from the basic elements of QC and IE. Since it was developed from the basics, it was flexible and could be applied

[1] Japan's prestigious award for quality, named for Dr. W. Edwards Deming, the American statistician who introduced quality control to the Japanese in the 1950s.

to a wide range of problems. However, to be useful this tool had to meet another requirement, specialization, which is the converse of flexibility. The tool also had to be tailored to the company's specific needs.

Thus the basics remain unchanged, but the means of applying them change to suit time and place. A tool must serve us. When we install a new piece of equipment, or use a newly bought jig or tool, we improve it if it does not work well in our plant. Likewise, since managerial engineering is a tool, it should be adapted to meet our specific needs in the best possible way.

As a member of the research and development staff at the beginning of my career, I had many opportunities to work at a variety of jobs. Before joining the IE Department, I had been in charge of designing new products and developing new equipment in the Technology Development Department. From my experiences as the new IE manager, I thought that the most important thing in managerial engineering was to develop our own methods, just as we did in other engineering disciplines.

We had to develop our own managerial systems, and make sure that they would be more useful and widely applicable in our company than the old methods. Developing these ideas would also stimulate us to conceive new ones.

Study groups were organized to develop this new managerial engineering. Small group activities involved employees from various levels of the corporate hierarchy and included both white and blue collar workers. (The activities and results of the first study group, known as the *Quality Control Problem Study Group*, will be discussed in Chapter 3.)

I recommend that the reader develop his own methods of managerial engineering by drawing on past experience and the ideas of all of his employees. A managerial system developed by a given company should be designed in terms of its specific business climate. This is especially true in the long run. If we seek only short-term results, we may find ways to solve quality and productivity problems. However, we must remember that measures which focus on short-term results may very well imperil the future of a company.

1.2   CREATING A FAVORABLE ENVIRONMENT

Even if we possess a reliable method, we can expect favorable results only if we establish the conditions necessary for its implementation.

In 1980, I visited Sumitomo Electric's overseas plants in Singapore, Thailand and Nigeria. Naturally, working conditions in those plants differed greatly from what I knew in Japan.

In January 1980, Sumitomo Electric started the Prosperity Through Cooperation (PTC) program. It was a three-year project, headed by the vice president, which aimed at setting up a system for producing better quality goods at lower costs, with faster delivery than our competitors. To reach this target, the company directed its efforts towards improving communications and strengthening ties with its suppliers. The philosophy behind the project was that both parties should benefit through cooperation. As IE manager, I was responsible for promoting the PTC.

The most important part of this project was to communicate its purpose to all the employees affected. We launched a publicity campaign using posters, company magazines, etc. We publicized the purpose of the program, its guiding principles and the important points that needed to be respected for its implementation. Meanwhile, I began by visiting the top management of each subcontractor to explain our goals to them. I was astonished to learn that some of our departments were working with companies located very far away. Sometimes when we visited those companies we were ushered into the president's house adjacent to the factory. In those cases, their offices were too small to accommodate even our small group. We spent much time on these visits because I felt that misunderstanding of our real purpose could sabotage our goals.

The first thing I understood when we began our tour was that most of the subcontractors lacked an environment suitable to work improvement activities. Some presidents showed anxiety or doubt about our presence. One said, for example: "You came to see our workshop. Please take a close look. Every single worker is doing his job without resting. They work very hard from morning to night. Where in this factory do you see room for improvement? It is very difficult for us even to find the spare time for any worker group activities."

Another said: "We employed a suggestion system as your company recommended. Well, I won't have anything more to do with it. All that I got from it was complaints about work and demands for new equipment. I lost interest in it. Before giving the workers incentives to perform better jobs, prove to me that this policy would improve productivity. In my factory, the products are made by machines. I am not interested in any kind of management system."

Indeed, we saw many workers literally working by the sweat of their brows under unshaded lamps. One said: "I, myself, went to several seminars on QC and IE. But I have never encountered a technique which meets our needs. I think those management techniques may be good for large firms, but not for us."

These reactions were so extreme that we felt helpless. While we listened to their opinions, spoken politely but with candor, we clearly understood that the tough situation of the suppliers would not allow us to introduce any managerial improvements unless we could make them appear exceptionally attractive. We had to find a breakthrough. After seriously re-

considering the matter, the managerial staff of our IE department came up with a fresh idea that had never been used. We
would go to the workshops of each subcontractor and actually
demonstrate how to improve work right on the spot, in front of
the president and the other people in the company. The first
day we would observe how the work was being done. On the
following morning, we would do some of the work in our improved way.

Company E in Osaka was the first subcontractor to be approached for this experiment. From among the many jobs we
observed, we chose simple ones to demonstrate our methods.
That night we met at the Sumitomo clubhouse and rehearsed
the jobs for the following day. I was given the role of a table. My
duty was just to stand quite still, holding a tray neatly covered
with tools, alongside the other members who were going to act
as operators. This was a wise role in which to cast me; I was too
clumsy to handle the machine.

The next morning, the president, engineering manager,

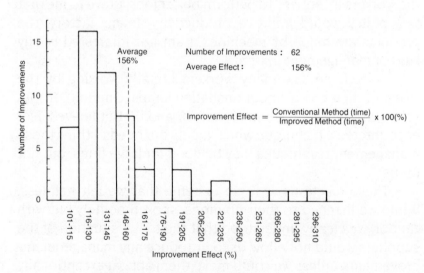

Figure 1-2 Results of Work Improvement

plant manager and other staff came to see our demonstration. We did four jobs. The first was tool setting for the milling machine. When we observed this task a day earlier, the operator had taken thirty-seven minutes, even though he worked hard under the added pressure of our cameras and stop watches. To our great amazement, we were able to perform his task in thirteen minutes.

We decided to present a note of gratitude to each worker who had allowed us to experiment on his job. The note said:

Dear Mr. _____ :

Thank you for your cooperation in our experiment. We were able to shorten the operating time by 64% and lighten the labor by arranging the tools properly, thus eliminating unnecessary motion. This is the basis of IE. Since you have been doing this work every day, we are confident that you will be able to improve it even more than we did once you learn the basics of IE.

There are infinite opportunities for improvement, even in well established factories. Best wishes for your health and work improvement.

Thank you,

IE Department
Sumitomo Electric

We found that the situation of the subcontractors improved markedly after the demonstration. We continued to visit the companies upon request. Partial results of the first sixty-two visits are shown in Figure 1-2.

On the first day of these visits, people tended to say: "We have already tried the method you are talking about, but it didn't work," or "We understand your point, but it is difficult for us to do so." However, they stopped saying so on the following day, after witnessing our demonstration. They usually showed strong interest in reliable methods and the basics of IE. One president later said: "The night of your visit, I could not sleep, thinking about what you had been able to do. The impact of your demonstration on me was somewhat akin to Commodore Perry's first visit to Japan in 1853, ending her two centuries of isolation."

As shown in Figure 1-2, the effect of work improvement varied from 10 to 310% with an average of 156%. The old "conventional method" is the numerator of the formula. It gives the operating time of the subcontractor's worker. The denominator ("improved method") is the time the task required using our methods. It is true that the workers in those companies work very hard, but the results indicate that their operation time can be reduced by 56% if basic IE techniques are used. The important point is that we increased productivity 56% by eliminating waste, not by accelerating operation speed. With our experience and the data from this experiment, we concluded that improvement must make work easier and more efficient.

Another factor to be stressed is that a 56% reduction was made against the value-added time. When only the incidental work, which is less than 20% of the total work, is targeted to be shortened, the workers will feel that the IE engineer is making their work harder by tightening up their schedule. Through demonstrations, we were able to communicate to workers that our intention was to ease everyone's work and lower costs.

Seeing the acceptance of our demonstration for the subcontractors, we developed an IE course as part of the PTC program. The course consisted of three eight-hour classes which presented the basic techniques of IE, tailored to our own needs. It was available to the employees both of our own company and of our subcontractors. In effect, we had discovered a critical fact: education is one of the most important

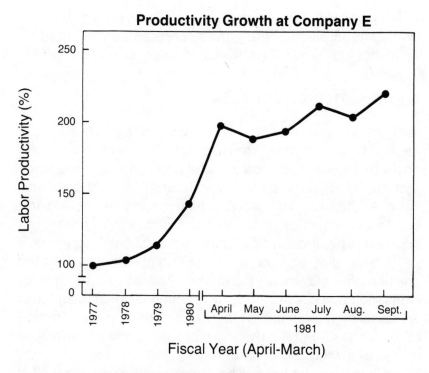

Figure 1-3 Productivity Growth at Company E

factors for creating a favorable environment.

Figures 1-2 and 1-3 show the growth of labor productivity in Company E, the first company we visited. This company secured a 40% improvement in productivity in less than a year (from 1980 to 1981). What is more, this was achieved at almost no added expense. I have introduced this example not to boast about our success, but to show that anyone can do this. Any company can establish an effective managerial system if it follows the basic principles of IE and develops a reliable method suited to its own production conditions. The only other requirement is practicing the method regularly.

I would like to emphasize that IE techniques are not

something only a few experts can use. IE was born to be used by anyone, anywhere. It is a warm science, based upon humanity. It should not be used to threaten or embarrass anyone.

1.3 PRACTICING TOGETHER

In Figure 1-1, point C says: "Keep all workers practiced in the method." For example, we were able to successfully demonstrate jobs at the subcontractors' because we frequently "got our hands dirty" on the shop floor of our own company. Furthermore, we had read and heard many reports on improvement activities. Thus we had unconsciously practiced floor level operations, and accumulated first-hand experience.

I rarely play golf, but when I talk to my friends about the practice of management techniques, I usually tease them by citing their practice in golfing. Where management techniques are concerned, perhaps the word "training" is more common than "practice." I prefer the word "practice," however, because it implies a voluntary effort of will.

When you want to learn how to play golf, you will probably go out and buy a "how-to" book or take lessons. Then you hit a ball for the first time. If your shot is poor, what will you think? Will you blame the book? Where golfing is concerned, people usually do not blame the book for their poor shots. Instead, they modestly regret their insufficient practice. After work or on a weekend, they go to a driving range and practice.

On the other hand, people tend to spend little effort on fully understanding a manual on management techniques, or they abandon techniques that do not work on the first try. Then they look for another manual. If the second one is not good, they seek something new without practicing. With this sort of attitude, how can they ever hope to perfect their management techniques?

In fact, I once bought a book called *Miracle Golfing*. However, my golfing skills have not improved at all. That is simply because I do not practice faithfully. The necessary conditions for victory in managerial engineering are:

- Developing a reliable method
- Creating a favorable environment for the method
- Improving everyone's skill with it through constant practice

Looking for powerful management techniques without the benefit of a reliable method is like playing a game with constantly changing rules. Winning such a game would be nothing short of a miracle.

The proper amount of (A + B + C) in Figure 1-1 determines the degree of success in implementing a project. Whenever we start a new project, we can foresee our chance of success by asking those three questions: Do we have a reliable method? Is the environment favorable? Is everyone familiar with the method? If the answers are negative, what right do we have to expect success?

According to my experience, one of the most important considerations is that (A + B + C) be a little bit greater than required. When the group's driving power (A + B + C) is greater than the difficulties that must be overcome, it can win.

I divide management power into three factors because this facilitates analyzing the situation. For instance, suppose we have accomplished Project I in six months. This means that our present situation of A, B and C is better than it was six months ago. We have made progress towards developing a reliable method. The environment has been getting better. We have practiced the method repeatedly. What took a week the first time now takes an hour. A setup that took hours can now be performed in minutes. Since we have grown as a group, we are now capable of attacking Project II, a more ambitious one than our first project.

By following these steps, we will achieve the projected

goal, and at the same time, we will build our strength. There may be strategies for attacking projects which require more power than we have, and even if it is possible to achieve a higher goal with extra effort, we may be exhausted. In view of the results we achieve, the difference between two strategies may appear insignificant. But no matter how small it may be, that difference is still there. Since success in the long run may be measured by a narrow margin, it is always important to maintain our competitive advantage.

Chapter 2

RELIABLE WORK

2.1 LESSONS LEARNED FROM ACCIDENTS

In 1972, I was working at the Facilities Development Section of Itami Works. It was divided into two sub-sections. Facilities Planning and Testing was responsible for developing and testing new equipment as well as planning and designing production facilities. Its responsibilities covered everything from purchasing materials to installation. The other sub-section was the Maintenance Department, which was in charge of preventive maintenance and repairs. It was broken down into two groups: the electric maintenance group and the mechanical maintenance group.

In the electric maintenance group there was a hydrogen squad whose duties included checking hydrogen gas purity upon receiving the gas from a tank truck, depressurizing and supplying the gas to hydrogen gas tanks, and further depressurizing and supplying the gas to three plants and one laboratory. The squad had not had an accident since its foundation, more than twenty years earlier.

In spite of this excellent record, I realized, as I watched the television news report of a tragic Japan Railways disaster at the

13

Hokuriku Tunnel, that we had to improve the squad's work quality.

Two points made by the news commentator drew my attention:

(1) When the driver noticed that the train had caught on fire, he stopped it in the middle of the tunnel. Why didn't he drive out into the open air?

(2) There were about twenty employees on duty in the train, including those who were working in the dining and mail coaches. However, only a few of them actually tried to fight the fire or lead the passengers to safety.

The first statement was obviously an afterthought of the commentator. Common sense suggested bringing the train to a full stop as soon as a fire broke out. The driver must not have been taught that he should drive the train out of a tunnel and then stop if a fire broke out. He had probably not been given the chance to think about such an occurrence in his daily work.

And if such an accident had occurred with the hydrogen at our plant.... Had we taught the people in charge the necessary emergency procedures?

Concerning the second point, I wondered whether the other people in the plant — the maintenance workers and users of hydrogen — would be able to help the hydrogen squad if an emergency were to occur. Probably not. We had not trained those people to do so.

We had to consider our firm's responsibility to society. No matter how good our business performance was, if the hydrogen exploded, we might very well lose everything. (Unfortunately, this thought was subsequently verified in the experience of another company.)

When I arranged the order of our jobs according to the required reliability, I realized that the highest priority should be given to the prevention of a possible hydrogen disaster.

Although I strongly felt the need for emergency measures and training, I didn't know where to begin.

2.2 DRIVEN BY NECESSITY

At that time, I was reading the Japanese translation of *Loud and Clear; The Full Answer to Aviation's Vital Question: Are Jets Really Safe?*, a book by Robert J. Serling (Doubleday & Co., New York, 1969), which reviewed many airplane accidents. On the surface these cases seemed unrelated to our work, but I attempted to find a common thread and glean some hints from it. I tried hard to find a breakthrough, and I did learn many lessons from the book. The Appendix to this chapter gives some of them.

Based on these hints from *Loud and Clear*, and with the cooperation of both the hydrogen squad and the plant's gas users, we wrote a pamphlet entitled *Emergency Procedures for Unforeseen Hydrogen Accidents*. It listed all the possible unexpected accidents we could imagine and suggested concrete countermeasures for each case.

In May 1973, this pamphlet was distributed to all sections. In it we described the necessity of preventing hydrogen disasters.

We also provided emergency training. While conducting this training, we made the very thought of disaster taboo, but stressed that if a disaster should occur, we would somehow be able to fight it. We tested each procedure, then trained our people over and over again. In doing so, I often encountered situations which made me think that if we didn't do something about the present state of affairs, we wouldn't be able to handle a real emergency. I was very much relieved that we had started this training.

The next step was to organize a special squad responsible for assisting the hydrogen squad in case of accidents. For the special squad, five top persons were selected from other maintenance groups. We began the education and training of the squad. We trained five people to a level that would allow them to work as efficiently as the members of the hydrogen squad, were an accident to occur.

In the process of training the new members, both the members of the hydrogen squad and I realized how differently their work appeared when observed in detail. Among the various ways of doing the work, there must be one best one for preventing hydrogen disasters.

The hydrogen squad spontaneously set about standardizing its work and eventually established the operations standards for twenty-four different jobs. As far as I knew, this was the first voluntary activity of its kind. What had driven them to create these standards and then train themselves to apply them? Was it a strong desire to find the best possible way of preventing accidents?

From these experiences, I learned the following:

(1) Exhortation alone is useless. "The duties of the hydrogen squad are important, so do your best." I, too, had often subjected employees to such advice. When I began this project to establish concrete prevention measures, I realized for the first time how useless these phrases are in practice.

(2) I learned what work standards really meant. Later on, when I started work as corporate IE manager, I set up a standardization study group (the Quality Control Problem Study Group).

2.3 EXTRACTING THE ESSENCE

In addition to these two lessons, I learned something even more important. I began to think in the abstract. The know-how for preventing hydrogen disasters came from studying airplane accidents. I think it is critical to be able to abstract the essence from the bare facts.

The word "abstract" is often viewed unfavorably in the business world. People often say: "Don't speak in such an abstract way; be specific." In this case however, I want to use the word in the sense of extracting an essence. When we see or hear something different from our daily work, we need to be able to extract its essence as a possible hint for solving our problems. It will become more and more vital for us businessmen to become skilled in extracting the essence. When we are close to the top and still want to learn from others, we have to be good at this skill. Furthermore, I believe that the ability to extract an essence is crucial to the development of new techniques in managerial engineering.

I noticed an interesting phenomenon. When we as a group visited another factory, shop-floor workers easily found common points with their own work and learned from them, even though the jobs looked quite different at first glance. On the other hand, white collar workers tend only to look at the different points. They say: "We are manufacturing the same kind of product, but ours is smaller than theirs. That is different. The functions of this machine are similiar to ours, but from a professional viewpoint I see there are differences between the two, I cannot learn from it."

What is the difference between these two approaches? Analysis and integration of facts are basic to IE. Both the blue and white collar workers are observing analytically. The fundamental difference lies in whether they can unite the analytically observed individual fact with a common thread. I believe that finding these common threads is professional work in a real sense.

2.4 TAKING A NEW LOOK AT HUMAN ERRORS

In 1973 a series of disasters, especially at petrochemical complexes, occurred in Japan. It was reported in the press that the causes of these disasters were human errors. I gathered as many detailed reports on the accidents as I could. Reviewing the reports, I strongly felt the necessity of preventive measures for avoiding human errors. Of course, emergency measures are important, but countermeasures against human error are important as well, since a human error in daily work might very well trigger a serious accident. This concern led us to develop a new project.

We began by clarifying the potential dangers in our work processes. Then we went on to find ways of preventing potential accidents. We made checklists according to each work process. Our aim was to establish fail-safe systems for possibly poorly designed operations or human errors. We reviewed all points of motion and checked every step in operations. Table 2-1 is an example. Looking back on it today, I feel that it includes several primitive and inadequate points, but it is the table we used at that time.

While carrying out this project, we made more than thirty improvements in tools, machines and operating methods. We clearly perceived where we had to focus our training efforts. IE engineers, mechanical designers and architectural designers participated in the project, and through our group effort, we gradually learned what reliability engineering was all about. I would like to stress that we learned from practice, driven by necessity, not from textbooks.

Since I had learned so much from *Loud and Clear*, I continued to read books about airplane accidents. Among my readings were *Mahha No Kyofu* (*Panic at Mach* 1) and *Zoku Mahha No Kyofu* (*After the Panic at Mach* 1) by Kunio Yanagida, published by Fujishuppansha. I obtained much information from these books. What conditions contribute to human error in a given system? What are the major points we should analyze? The following are examples of what I learned:

- Stress and tension (theory of errors)
- Purpose of verifying meters
- No two accidents occur in the same way
- Redundant design function does as intended
- Heinrich's principles (information flow for minor accidents)
- The use of fail-safe systems

OPERATION	MOTION	CHECK POINTS	POTENTIAL DANGER FROM MIS-HANDLING A = critical B = serious C = slight	PREVENTIVE MEASURES
1. Post a warning signal card	Place card manually	Post at specified place	B	Put up a double guard
2. Guide the tank truck	Guide driver with hand signals	Watch area behind truck	A	Put a safety fence around area
3. Stop the truck	Blow stop whistle	Test whistle beforehand	A	Put a safety barrier around area and around ignition key
4. Block the wheels	Place blocks	Put blocks under rear wheels	A	Put two blocks behind each rear wheel
5. Ground	Connect grounding clip	Verify that clip is secure	A	
6. Attach connecting pipe	Fasten pipe with safety tool	Verify that only 2/3 of each screw's thread is fastened and that there are no gas leaks in pipe	B	
7. Make sure holder valve is closed	Check that valve is closed		B	
8. Open main valve of truck	Open valve slowly by hand	Check gas flow at valve	B	Use a gas detector
9. Purge air from connecting pipe	Open blow valve to release air slowly	Check gas flow and post warning signal card	B	
10. Open pressure gauge valve	Open valve completely, then close a little		C	

Table 2-1 Potential Dangers in an Operation

It is said that approximately 60% of all airplane accidents are caused by human error. No matter how far technology advances, people are ultimately responsible for error-free operation. I am not saying that we, human beings, should take all responsibility for accidents. I mean that we should be fully aware that people do make errors and that we must construct machines and systems which take this fact into account. This experience later led to the founding of our Human Error Study Group.

While we were working aggressively on this project, an accident almost occurred. Mr. Umakichi Kurano of the hydrogen squad detected an abnormal flow of gas and took speedy action, thus preventing an accident which might have pulverized the entire plant.

One day I read in the newspapers that Mr. Kozo Kitamura had been studying gas explosions for the past twenty years. I asked him to come check our works. "In most companies," he commented, "more exciting work gets everyone's attention, and the dull jobs such as receiving and supplying hydrogen are relatively ignored. What makes you so active in this area?"

What if the abnormality detected by Mr. Kurano had taken place before we had started our work? At that time, all I could give the workers was an announcement saying: "The hydrogen squad has a great responsibility; do your best." When I wonder whether he would have been able to take appropriate actions under those circumstances, I break into a cold sweat. I cannot deny the relationship between what he did and the fact that his team was trained for these eventualities.

2.5 THE DAY THE "GRAY WORKSHOP" CHANGED

Lastly, through our hydrogen-disaster prevention experience, I learned the critical importance of motivation. Towards the end of the project, I came upon the members of the hydrogen squad making a model of the hydrogen distribution system, although I had not ordered them to do so. The model was so devised that everyone could see at a glance the flow of gas, the distribution of the pipes, and the function and location of the various meters and valves.

"Why did you make this magnificent model?" I asked them. They replied that in the event of an emergency, they would immediately call the people in charge of the three plants and the laboratory in front of the model. By using it, they would be better able to command the situation.

By that time, special telephones for use in emergencies had been installed. During the experiment it became evident that the regular telephones were not enough, because there were moments, especially during the night shift, when no one was available near the phones.

I was quite moved to witness this independent activity.

Were these the same people who used to go on in the same old rut in the section nicknamed the "Gray Workshop" because of its elderly workers? It was really an eye-opener. The Facilities Development Section was a part of the Technology Development Department. At the time the model was being developed, I was assistant manager of that department. We were not necessarily lacking in lively projects. Development of new products and facilities and construction of a new plant were also progressing. However, I believed that the prevention of potential hydrogen disasters was our most important mission.

This was not a reflection on the other projects. I simply felt that were an explosion to occur, it might result in the total disruption of our activities.

From this project I learned the essential conditions for motivation. Whatever the job may be, when people recognize its necessity and importance, and when the required measures are taken, they become highly motivated. This is a fact, not a theory.

In a good plant or shop, people should feel as excited as Paul Revere dashing through the night with his passion for revolution over two hundred years ago. What should I call it? Mission? Aspiration? I believe that the ultimate factor supporting quality work lies in each individual's mind: aspiration — something spontaneous.

APPENDIX TO CHAPTER 2
CONVERSION OF LESSONS FROM AIRCRAFT ACCIDENTS TO PREVENTIVE MEASURES AGAINST HYDROGEN ACCIDENTS [1]

On December 20, 1966, more than a year after the collision, the Civil Aeronautics Board issued a report which found an optical illusion responsible for the mishap. The CAB said the cloud bank just under the Constellation in reality sloped downward, giving White and Holt a false horizon. They actually were separated horizontally from the jet by the required one thousand feet — Eastern had been assigned to ten thousand feet and TWA to eleven thousand — but were fooled into thinking that TWA was at their altitude. Likewise, the TWA pilots also took evasion action because of an identical illusion — they assumed EAL 853 was at eleven thousand. The supreme irony was that the alertness of both crews triggered the collision. It would not have occurred if one or both had not spotted the other. (p. 68)

Altimeter trouble, either a malfunction of a misreading, could have been a factor in this accident and it may have played unsuspected roles in other crashes blamed on everything but the altimeter. (p. 140)

[1] Excerpts from *Loud and Clear*, see above, p. 15.

(Are our meters always reliable? If not, a person will instinctively rely on his judgment at the last moment.)

The NASA report to the CAB pretty well pinpointed the real reason for at least three of the four tragedies — failure in airline training programs to emphasize the virtues of the 727 as a potential hazard. Namely, that its ability to make short landings could also be a booby trap for any pilot who does not fly the 727 by the book. NASA informed the CAB that close-in, so-called "unstabilized" approaches with high rates of descent, were being conducted more often in the 727 than in any other jet transport. (p. 178)

(Likewise, we must consider the safety of new facilities with regard to hydrogen from the initial designing stage.)

The second lesson, however, was the direct result of the Salt Lake City accident — the tardy realization that passengers need better odds for getting out of a theoretically survivable crash. (p. 179)

(In plants, too, there must be ways to prevent a disaster resulting from a minor accident.)

"...the captain's voice came over the intercom and in a very reassuring manner he told us that if we would obey orders there was no need to panic; that everyone should put on his life jacket; take off shoes; place his pillow on his lap; and lean forward... He also told us to remove any sharp obstacles [he meant objects] and wrap our hands around our ankles." (p. 58)

(In case of hydrogen accident, who is going to be a commander? Is that person trained?)

The cabin was quiet: the six flight attendants — the purser and five stewardesses — had everything under control and ready for landing. (pp. 58-59)

"As one of those one hundred and seventy-four guinea pigs, I unfastened my belt and started stumbling through the smoke toward the rear — where I remembered boarding. (My reaction was typical of the majority of all airline passengers; I instinctively headed for the door through which I boarded, even though there was an emergency exit much closer.)" (p. 181)

(We have to get more information on human behavior in an emergency.)

C. Hayden LeRoy, an investigator for the CAB's Bureau of Safety, later did a thorough and valuable analysis of the evacuation flow, as well as other survival aspects of the UAL accident. His study provided an interesting correlation between the seat locations of surviving passengers and the exits they used. The majority followed an escape route toward the entrances used when boarding. In some cases, this contributed to the fatality toll, because a number of passengers were overcome by smoke and flames before they could reach exits at the opposite end of the plane. (p. 184)

Obviously, there is considerable "it always happens to the other guy but it could never happen to me" thinking on the part of the public or, for that matter, even of the part of some crew members. This ostrich attitude could be placed in the same category as smoking three packs of cigarettes daily or driving a car at sixty MPH after downing five martinis. It is a foolhardy attitude because no one can predict an accident and no one, even more significantly, can predict his own reactions if an accident occurs. (p. 184)

(Don't think that we can predict an accident. What we can think of is only a part of it. In reality, an accident attacks us suddenly in a way we could never predict.)

"You all know why you're here," Clancie [manager of steward-esses] began. "To make sure you know what to do in a few minutes or even seconds to assure the safety of the greatest number of passengers possible. And I mean seconds. If something goes wrong with no warning, you won't have time to look up procedures in your manual." (p. 201)

"All of you admitted you've never tried saying it aloud, in practice. Lock yourself in your bathroom if your roommate laughs at you. Don't trust to luck any phase of emergency procedures. The chances are that not a single girl of this room or in this base will ever have to make that PA. But this doesn't mean you shouldn't be prepared to make it." (p. 204)

Now the class proceeded to unplanned emergencies and the questions came at the girls like machine-gun bullets.

How do you handle an incapacitated passenger in a crash landing?... What do you do in case of an in-flight cabin fire?... Where are the emergency stations for the first stewardess...second...third?...

Then came the written test. Questions like:

During your briefing for a planned belly landing in a 727, where would you tell a passenger sitting in 19A to try to evacuate first?" (p. 204)

(Similar questions might be: You are on night shift, working at a hydrogen furnace. The south end furnace of the line has just gone up in a blast, the next one catches from the blast, and it seems as though explosions will continue in a line toward you. What would you do at the moment? Or: While you are filling

the hydrogen gas into a gas holder from a tank truck, the con-
necting pipe comes off, and the gas is blowing off violently. It
hasn't caught fire yet. What do you have to think of first? What
actions would you take immediately?)

Chapter 3

A RELIABLE METHOD (1): THE CAUSE AND EFFECT DIAGRAM WITH THE ADDITION OF CARDS

Improving product quality, decreasing variations in quality and reducing the defect rate are basic and essential tasks for manufacturing firms. In this age of low economic growth and keen competition, superior product quality has become a key source of competitive advantage. Since improving quality and reducing defects are essentially one and the same — the difference between the two lying in where one chooses to set quality standards and limits — we will approach the problem from the latter point of view for the sake of simplicity.

The term quality control, and the concepts it implies, are widely known throughout Japan. A few years ago, I was visiting a factory in the countryside on a hot summer day. On the way I stopped at a small restaurant and ordered iced noodles. When a young waitress appeared with the order, I commented that one of the bowls was cracked. She replied immediately: "QC for this bowl wasn't very good!" — a remarkable indication of how popularized QC has become in Japan.

3.1   IDEAL CONDITIONS

About seven years ago, we were looking for an effective method for reducing our defect rate. We were especially concerned with two kinds of defects: those for which we were unable to identify the cause, and those which were caused by the inability of our processes to achieve designed quality levels. These problems often appear in the early production stage of new products

When such defects appear, people often blame weaknesses in operation and engineering standards for the product. Since we did not yet know all of the causes of these defects, it was impossible for us to write truly effective and practical standards. First of all, we had to establish standard production techniques and operations. Whether or how they were to be described on paper was a secondary problem. We set our sights on creating an easy method that would allow everyone to develop and use standard techniques and operations.

We had also been annoyed by another QC standardization problem. The more our production process produced defects, the more we needed improvements in operations, manufacturing conditions and equipment. The revised standards never caught up with frequent improvements made in processes. Since no factory had excess manpower to assign to the task of revision, the standards remained perpetually out of date. Consequently, the differences between actual operations and official standards led workers to ignore the latter.

Timely revision of standards was also difficult in the following situation. When we effected an improvement in manufacturing equipment or conditions, we usually had to wait some time before we actually observed a decrease in defects. It was virtually impossible for us to update standards in our daily work after each of these improvement cycles. In many cases, no one bothered to revise them. We wanted a system by which

truly reliable standards were constantly provided and adhered
to by everyone.

Table 3-1 summarizes the above situation. It also describes the ideal conditions to be realized from an imperfect
production environment.

3.2   THE QUALITY CONTROL PROBLEM STUDY
GROUP — CONDITIONS FOR DEVELOPMENT

The Quality Control Problem Study Group was formed in
November 1975 under the direction of the Industrial Engineering Department. Its goal was to develop a method suitable for
securing the ideal conditions given in Table 3-1. I was appointed manager of this department in July of that year.

The group originally consisted of thirty-two volunteers
with various positions in the company — plant managers
(Sumitomo Electric has nearly forty plants), foremen, produc-

PRESENT CONDITIONS TO BE IMPROVED	IDEAL CONDITIONS TO BE ACHIEVED
1. We cannot decrease defects because we do not know effective standard methods and operations for achieving expected quality levels.	Before establishing standard operations on paper, deter-mine which manufacturing methods now in use are most effective.
2. In the production process, where effective standards are really needed, the revision of standards cannot keep up with the rapid improvements which are continuously being made.	When improvements are made, they must immediately be recorded as standards, and communicated and adhered to by everyone concerned.

Table 3-1   Purposes of Standardization

tion engineers, industrial engineers, etc. It included members
from the ranks of management, staff and blue collar employees. In other words, it was a small, vertically integrated circle. I
felt that such a formation was desirable for the development of
a new method.

The group was set up along the following principles:

(1) *Although we were working towards a single goal (ideal conditions), the thirty-two members were instructed to develop thirty-two distinct approaches.*

When faced with a difficult problem, the Japanese tend to
stick unswervingly to whatever idea they happen to hit upon.
By thus manifesting their determination, they expect to win
the sympathy and respect of others. I felt that it would be much
more useful to have each member work creatively on his own
individual proposals. Thus the group would benefit from a
variety of ideas.

(2) *Each member was to work on a problem drawn directly from his
daily work in the plant, for which he would develop and test his own method.
I asked each member to do this as though he were "nursing a young plant."*

Picking a problem from one's own work was simple but
critical. Choosing a problem that was very important for the
company, but did not come from his own work, could not work.
The main reason for this has to do with the member's motivation; I hoped the members would develop enough zeal to at-
tend the meetings assiduously. If attendance did help members with their own concrete problems, they would become
powerfully motivated. If, on the other hand, they were to deem
managerial engineering a further burden to their already
crowded schedules, they would give up easily. Managerial engineering must be a useful tool that helps us in our day-to-day
work.

I used the above image of "nursing a young plant" because each group member was required to bring the same
methods to problem solving as one uses to nurse a young

plant — knowledge and experience. Furthermore, once a month all the members brought their "plants" to the meetings to show to the others. By observing them and sharing know-how, each member could learn more. Our intention was to create a new method by integrating all this knowledge and experience. Even though each method in itself often contained nothing new, we created a new approach by integrating all these diverse methods and knowledge into a single, coherent approach.

Looking back on the beginning of the study group, I suppose the members may have had many doubts on their minds, such as: "The only reason the company called this group together is to impose standardization measures," or "Perhaps the new IE manager is going to tell us about his new ideas and then force us to use them."

Some of them may have attended the first meetings with resignation. They may have thought: "We have already tried many different methods and none of them have met our expectations. Our problems are really tough. Perhaps we shouldn't expect too much from this meeting, either."

Other members may have had ready-made explanations for their not being able to achieve ideal conditions. I made a point of explaining to members that since existing methods had proved inadequate, our goal would be to create new techniques for improving quality and productivity.

It is always difficult to start something truly new. In fact, we were quite anxious about how the group would turn out. An IE staff member confessed to me his initial feeling — that if the group was able to meet more than three times, that would already indicate a certain degree of success.

(3) *Meetings were held monthly at each of our five works, and the number of members attending each meeting was generally not more than ten.*

The members functioned as liaisons between the group

and the plants and also led QC activities in their respective plants. In this way we learned much about leadership, and we found that the positions of the members did not necessarily represent their levels of leadership activities in their plants.

(4) *The groups operated on the principle of open membership. This meant that anyone interested in a group could enter it freely, and anyone who was dissatisfied could leave.*

The number of people attending the meetings grew to almost 100. This number was not constant, however, since individuals were free to join or leave as they wished.

When I explained this study group approach to managers from other companies, they often expressed astonishment at our management's generosity in allowing the group members to devote company time to such a dubious enterprise. I would like to stress that it was this warm support both from management and from the line that enabled us to bring our project to fruition.

The study group developed a technique for improving quality and productivity — the Cause-and-Effect Diagram with the Addition of Cards (CEDAC®). Through this example, I hope the reader will understand my way of thinking and methodology for managerial engineering development.

This book is not meant to be used as a textbook of QC and IE. Furthermore, rather than bore the reader with abstract discussions, I cite actual cases, drawn from our experience at Sumitomo Electric and Meidensha Electric Mfg. Co., to illustrate theoretical ideas. My goal is to leave the reader with a sufficiently clear understanding that he may apply the principles to other situations. Even those managers who are not directly involved with QC or IE in production, such as marketing or personnel professionals, will thus understand not only the cases themselves, but their essence, and will be able to apply this understanding to the quality and productivity problems encountered in their own departments.

3.3   WHAT IS CEDAC?

CEDAC grew out of the diverse approaches of the individual group members. It is a modification of the cause-and-effect diagram, which was already well known and widely used by QC circles in our plants when I started our quality improvement project.

An example of the cause-and-effect diagram is given in Figure 3-1.

All the factors considered to be causes of a given effect are written out in "fish-bone" form. CEDAC grew out of this diagram. It emphasizes the importance of both the engineering knowledge and workers' practical experience that lie behind simple words such as "temperature" or "dryness" found on the cause-and-effect diagram.

However, the traditional cause-and-effect diagram uses single words, written at the appropriate place on the diagram, to indicate the causes of a given problem and their inter-relationships.

In order to solve a serious quality control problem, we must start at the very beginning, distinguishing what we know from what we do not know. For this purpose, a short sentence is more desirable than a single word to fully express what is known.

The use of small cards is another point. In traditional QC circle applications of cause-and-effect diagrams, the employees must wait until the weekly meeting to put their ideas on the chart. If people have to wait before they can get together to share information, they will often miss a timely opportunity to solve problems. It is usually very difficult to gather together all the workers on the shop floor.

Furthermore, people often feel very timid about writing their own ideas directly onto a wall diagram. If they do write, they tend to feel that they must express their ideas in a formal

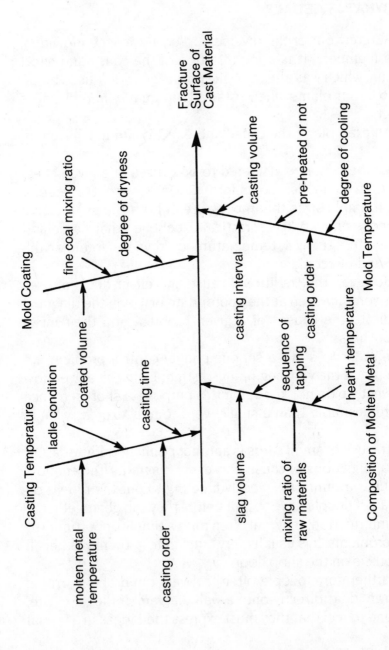

Figure 3-1 Cause-and-Effect Diagram

way. The use of cards solves both of these problems at one stroke. Each worker is free to jot down an idea whenever it enters his mind.

The use of cards also facilitates revision of the diagram, since a new card can be pinned on top of the corresponding old one. The succession of cards at any given point on the chart may thus be interpreted as a history of changes occurring at a specific point in the production process.

Most statistical quality control methods integrate quantitative information, but there is also a lot of important qualitative information available in the plant which is either non-quantifiable or not yet quantified. CEDAC is a tool that allows the quality circle to integrate this kind of information. Raw information is indispensable for problem solving not only in manufacturing, but also in marketing, personnel and in other fields. Such information often evaporates quickly, leaving only a minor numerical trace.

Once when I was learning about a control chart at a QC seminar, the instructor gave us an assignment to draw a control chart using numerical data in our own plants. In fact, I found it very difficult because there was little numerical data available in our plant which could be meaningfully written on a control chart.

It was my hope that CEDAC could be used to gather together the ideas of many people by comparing causes and effects, especially in those cases where qualitative information plays a critical role. CEDAC encourages the exploration of both favorable and unfavorable causes and looks for the effects and relations between them by permitting the systematic analysis of facts.

The following paragraphs describe the application of CEDAC to the manufacturing process. The basic principles and techniques of CEDAC remain the same in other business applications. The reader is encouraged to interpret the rest of this book according to his own needs.

3.4 STEPS FOR IMPLEMENTING THE CEDAC SYSTEM

Figure 3-2 shows the basic structure of CEDAC. These five steps are used to implement the CEDAC system:

(1) Select a major quality problem that you want to solve and specify the goal to be achieved. It is important to specify the quality quantitatively, although this is not always easy.

(2) Write out all technical know-how and manufacturing conditions that are thought to have an influence on quality. From this, a selection of the needed information is made by workers, production engineers, plant engineers and all other concerned persons. Put all of this information in diagram form.

(3) Hang the diagram on a wall of the plant for all to see. This way, the causes and effect to be studied will be visible to everyone.

(4) When quality cannot be kept within control limits,

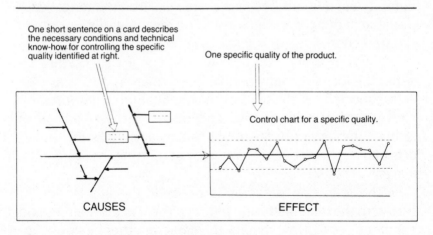

One short sentence on a card describes the necessary conditions and technical know-how for controlling the specific quality identified at right.

One specific quality of the product.

Control chart for a specific quality.

CAUSES

EFFECT

Figure 3-2 Basic Structure of CEDAC

room for improvement in the causes is indicated. Thus, the root of the problem is sought through the gathering of more facts. If necessary, the group tests its tentative countermeasure for the problem, then observes and analyzes the results.

(5) Based on the analysis of Step (4), the group will decide to make improvements either in technique or equipment. The exact nature of this improvement is written down on a card which is then pinned on top of the corresponding old card. As a group of cards is gradually accumulated, it will show not only the past record of the production process, but also the effects of each improvement.

Everyone participates in the process from Steps (2) to (5). With such a method, previously unknown information is discovered, and necessary improvements are made on a step by step basis, without any regression.

In Step (1), a major quality problem must be selected. It has been my experience that everyone concerned must do his best in order to create anything really new. Groups using CEDAC for the first time often make the mistake of choosing an easy rather than a difficult problem. This leads to a very high risk of failure, because the group members can only obtain insignificant inspiration and results by tackling a minor problem. It is essential to tackle the most serious problem that everyone is eager to solve.

The cause-and-effect diagram was used as the basis of CEDAC. This is not only because it was already being widely used throughout the company. More importantly, cause-and-effect diagrams became the basis of CEDAC because it is essential to analyze quality control problems in terms of cause and effect.

However, we decided not to stick to the fish-bone form of diagram. With the permission of Professor Kaoru Ishikawa, inventor of the cause-and-effect diagram, we were able to use any diagram as long as it clearly expressed causes and effects.

Regarding Step (2), Figure 3-3 shows the process of incorporating various bits of data. First of all, cards are collected from all the group members.

The cards will often show a variety of approaches. When an existing operational standard is not sufficiently good to prevent defects from appearing, workers will not necessarily observe it; they may try different approaches in order to decrease the number of defects. It is not important to know how these standards are described on paper. In fact, it is not even necessary to describe these standards on paper at all. The important issue is whether procedures or standards effective enough to produce the desired quality are known or not.

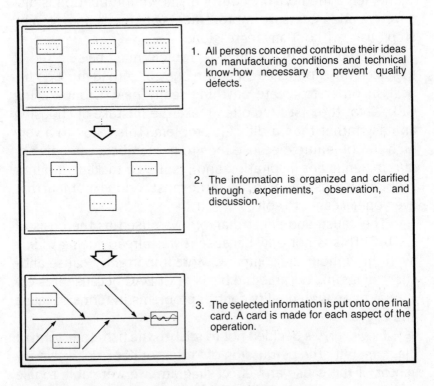

1. All persons concerned contribute their ideas on manufacturing conditions and technical know-how necessary to prevent quality defects.

2. The information is organized and clarified through experiments, observation, and discussion.

3. The selected information is put onto one final card. A card is made for each aspect of the operation.

Figure 3-3 Process of Incorporating Data on Cards

For instance, Operator A happened to experiment with a new method during a rainy night shift. He observed that this method produced zero defects and has adhered to it ever since. Quite naturally, he told it to Operator B. Unfortunately, Operator B missed a few important details when he attempted to use the same method himself. When they wrote their respective methods down on cards, it became clear to both workers that they had overlooked differences on critical points.

Another typical example is the production engineer who discovered that workers were following methods completely different from those that he had established for them. This discovery led him to revise his current experiments and plans to take into account these discrepancies.

Thus, in many ways, management and engineering are inevitably confronted by the great variety in workers' methods and know-how. At Sumitomo Electric we observed that this variability often causes serious quality control problems. The great power of the CEDAC method lies in its ability to integrate all of the information concerning this variability on a single card through fact-finding, QC circle meetings and experiments (Figure 3-3).

An important point concerning Step (4) is that looking for a cause after a given abnormality has been spotted by a control chart is not as effective or practical as observing effects by making changes in the causes. Note that these changes may be made intentionally or unintentionally, but always consciously.

The latter approach brings more accurate, timely and appropriate information with less time and effort. It also enables us to obtain information on what factors affect quality and what factors do not change it at all. Moreover, it is a much more interesting and stimulating approach, which is an important factor in our daily work.

CAUSE

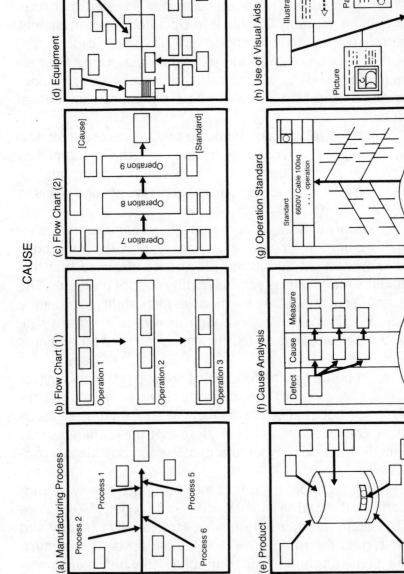

(a) Manufacturing Process

(b) Flow Chart (1)

(c) Flow Chart (2)

(d) Equipment

(e) Product

(f) Cause Analysis

(g) Operation Standard

(h) Use of Visual Aids

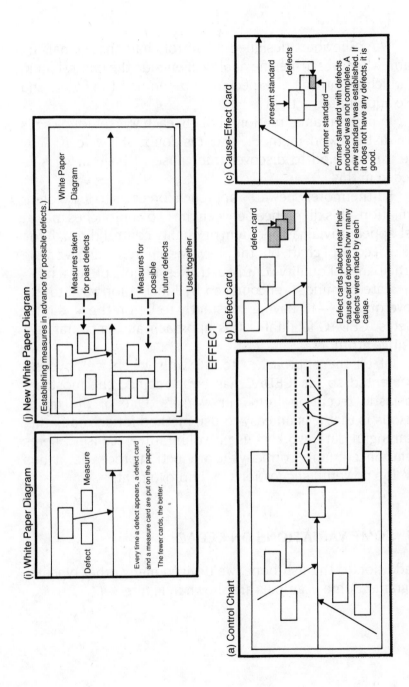

Figure 3-4 Some Variations of CEDAC

W.A. Shewhart designed a control chart that signals an alarm whenever a specific quality is outside the control limit, at which point one is expected to determine the cause and take appropriate action.

In a real plant situation, though, each worker follows his own distinct work methods, and it is doubtful if we can really use this method to discover true causes. I have never succeeded in this.

Furthermore, Shewart's approach forces us to look for information. This difference between the two approaches may at first appear trivial, as both aim at quality control through the use of a control chart, but they have far different effects on the participants of quality control activities. People prefer a positive state of mind — encouraged by looking for ways to improve quality — to having constantly to be on the watch for defects. CEDAC facilitates this approach and encourages a positive attitude.

Of all the approaches to QC with which we have experimented so far, CEDAC has by far gained the most enthusiastic reception from our workers. One of the major reasons is that it is an easy-to-use method for accumulating meaningful data; workers use it voluntarily because it helps them conceptualize correctly the production process, and thus develop powerful suggestions for improvements.

3.5 SOME VARIATIONS ON CEDAC

In addition to the fish-bone, we devised many other types of diagrams. Some examples are shown in Figure 3-4.

3.6   THE CONCEPTUAL FRAMEWORK OF CEDAC

As shown in Figure 3-4, CEDAC has taken on a great variety of forms and functions developed by members of the Quality Control Problem Study Group to meet their respective needs and backgrounds. However, all of these variations share a common conceptual framework, which is shown in Figure 3-5.

As (i) of Figure 3-5 indicates, the workers group is in the most advantageous position for fact-finding. This is so because:
• They are constantly observing raw facts
• Their sheer number helps in fact-finding
• Their accumulated years of experience have led them to acquire tremendous insight into the production process

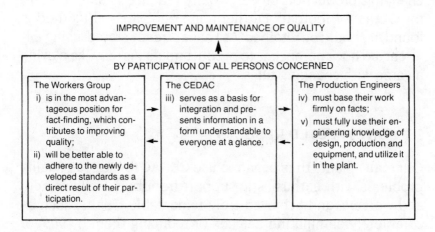

Figure 3-5   The Basic Conceptual Framework of CEDAC

- They get their hands dirty in their work, and have a great
  desire to solve the problems they encounter on a day-to-
  day basis

People tend to underestimate the basic fact-finding function of all QC circle activity. CEDAC highlights this function,
which is one of the great strengths of workers, and aims at the
systematic integration of facts observed by individual workers.

On the other hand, production engineers possess engineering knowledge that can help them discover the causes of
defects. All too often today, factual information provided by
workers is allowed to evaporate into mere tables of numerical
data. This information must be used by engineers to significantly improve operations by discovering unknown factors
and developing improvement ideas.

The use of CEDAC, if adequately practiced, facilitates the
solution of the many problems which crop up in the constantly
changing production process. Daily practice is as important
for QC as for football. Furthermore, once a good method is
found, it should be retained. As I have already stated, using different, ad hoc approaches to product quality is just like playing
a game with changing rules.

3.7 UNEXPECTED RESULTS

Our many plants thus began to use CEDAC for serious quality
problems with enthusiastic support from both management
and workers, and achieved truly remarkable results, such as
completely eliminating defects, or reducing them by 90% or
more.

Table 3-2 summarizes the results obtained in two of our
plants where all of the workers groups tried the CEDAC approach on a total of thirty-one QC problems. The results were
obtained within periods of four days to eight months. In about

Problems \ Results	Excellent (more than 90% decrease in percent of defects)	Very Good (50-90% decrease in percent of defects)	Fair (less than 50% decrease in percent of defects)	Total number of problems
Dealt with by engineers but unsolved	1	5	0	6
Dealt with by worker group	5	3	1	9
Not dealt with at all	10	2	4	16
Total number of problems	16	10	5	31
Percentage	52%	32%	16%	100%

Table 3-2   Results of Applying CEDAC

half of the cases, defects decreased by more than 90%, which far surpassed our original expectations.

When we plotted the results on a graph, we also observed an interesting pattern of changes in the percentage of defects. In many cases, the curve dropped suddenly and drastically, and then leveled off without any further regression. Such a pattern had never been observed in prior QC activities.

The members of our study group were excited. CEDAC is merely a simple modification of the cause-and-effect diagram, and at the outset we only expected it to produce an easier method for revising standards. We were unable to explain why it produced such remarkable results. We decided to investigate the reason since we were not satisfied by simply achieving good results; we wanted to understand the mechanism by which QC problems are solved. Our members became increasingly enthusiastic.

3.8   LESSONS FROM THE HAWTHORNE STUDY

To analyze the effectiveness of CEDAC, we applied research principles learned from the famous study which was made about fifty years ago at the Hawthorne Works of Western Electric Company, Chicago, Illinois. With the development of statistical methods and the computer, our analytical techniques are far more sophisticated today. What we learned from this study was not the techniques, but rather a basic research attitude necessary for managerial engineering.

Putting aside our CEDAC story for a while, a short explanation of the illumination experiments which were part of the Hawthorne study is in order. From 1924 to 1933 Western Electric conducted research and experiments on the factors that influence worker morale and productivity. The illumination experiments were the first part of the Hawthorne study. They were conducted by management in conjunction with the National Research Committee of the National Academy of Sciences. The study was led by Elton Mayo of Harvard University and others. It is said that the study was so extensive that it produced several tons of documents.

The goal of these experiments was to measure the relationship between lighting and productivity. In the experiments five women were selected from many female workers of the relay assembly room and transferred to an experiment room. It was originally expected that decreasing the level of illumination would decrease productivity. However, the results were not all that simple. Contrary to expectations, productivity increased. Productivity only decreased when the room was too dark to see anything at all. The experiment itself was considered a failure.

However, it is to the Hawthorne experimenters' credit that they perceived the existence of unknown factors behind this unexpected increase in the women's productivity in spite of the fact that they were working in a darkened room. It has been said that this inquisitive attitude has opened up new frontiers in engineering, such as motivation theory, organizational behavior, etc. And it is this attitude that we should adopt in managerial science whenever we hit upon an unexpected phenomenon: wondering about it, looking for causes and analyzing its mechanism.

The Hawthorne study was published as a book which introduces the five young women complete with pictures and very detailed biographical data such as the national origins of their parents. Even the menus of their breakfasts before each experiment were recorded. From the wealth of such data it becomes clear that the researchers were trying to approach the problem as scientifically as possible.[1]

We decided to apply this attitude. By finding a scientific explanation to our own unexpected discovery — the far-reaching effects of CEDAC — we were able to develop a reliable method that can be applied by anyone, any time, anywhere.

3.9   THE HYPOTHESIS OF NEW JOHARRY'S WINDOW

Returning to the remarkable effectiveness of CEDAC (Table 3-2), here we present a hypothesis we formulated to explain it.

As Figure 3-6 shows, Joharry's Window was used by Joseph Luft and Harry Ingram to describe communication between two persons ("you" and "I"):

- Category I refers to what both you and I know
- Category II refers to what I know and you do not know

---

[1] It became clear to us that the statistical analysis of the Hawthorne study may contain certain errors; this point will be discussed in Chapter 8.

I \ You	Know	Don't Know
Know	I	II
Don't Know	III	IV

Figure 3-6   Joharry's Window

- Category III refers to what you know and I do not know
- Category IV refers to that which neither knows

Although Ruft and Ingram used this model to explain the internal conditions of the mind, it gave us an important clue as to the importance of CEDAC's effectiveness. We modified the window as shown in Figure 3-7, and considered our hypothesis as follows.

First, let me explain the New Joharry's Window.

(1) The different categories represent the interrelationship of the counterparts *Section* A and *Section* B. These terms can be used to refer to individuals, groups, teams, sections within the organization, etc.

(2) In the *known-practiced* column, the respective party already knows the right methods to prevent defects and executes them correctly.

(3) In the *known-unpracticed* column, the respective party knows the right method but executes them insufficiently or not at all.

(4) In the *unknown* column, the respective party does not yet know the right methods to prevent defects.

(5) In *Category* I, everyone in both parties knows and correctly practices the best and most effective operation known at any given time. All standard operations must be included in this category.

(6) In *Category* II, everyone in both parties is informed of

Step 1
Define the standard operation clearly and communicate it to all concerned.

Step 2
Put into correct practice the established standard operation.

Step 3
Improve the manufacturing method if a satisfactory quality level is not yet achieved.

Step 4
Revise the standard operation.

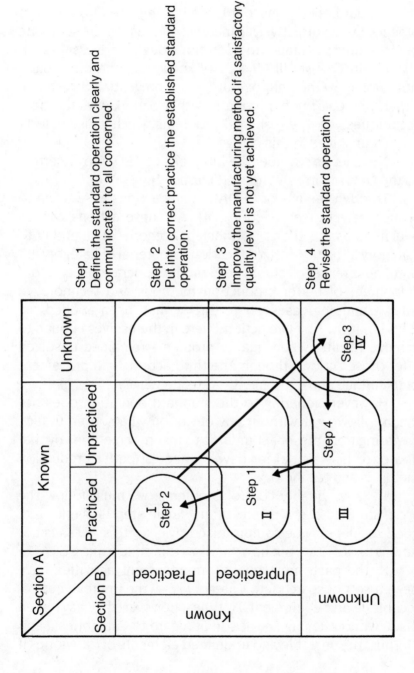

Figure 3-7 New Joharry's Window

the standard operations, but there is someone who does not practice them correctly. This includes the case where someone fails to adhere to standard operations out of carelessness.

(7) In *Category* III, one party knows but the other party does not know the right operations for preventing defects.

(8) In *Category* IV, no one in either party knows the right techniques yet. The technical problems which cause defects remain unsolved in this category.

Next, let us consider the functions of CEDAC by referring to the New Joharry's Window (Figure 3-7).

Through the use of CEDAC, many actions were taken to reduce defects (see Section 3.4). All these actions can be explained as the efforts to transfer Categories II, III and IV to Category I. That is, "communication of material in Category III," then "adherence to established standard operations" and "development of better production methods and technology." After examining cases where CEDAC had been applied, we found that the first two actions were in themselves enough to achieve results. When quality problems remained unsolved after those actions, though, the third action — improvement of technique and equipment — was necessary.

However, adhering to the standard operation does not mean following it without any deviation whatsoever. In fact, deviating from present standards to test new methods by trial and error is essential for development of better production methods and technology.

To solve quality control problems, we must follow the cycle Steps 1, 2, 3, 4, 1, etc. If any single step is overlooked, good results may be compromised. The key to success is not how to use CEDAC, but how to follow this cycle using CEDAC.

In the past, most quality improvement activities have been a sort of search into Category IV — the improvement of technique and equipment. At times, however, they have been made without taking any action in regard to Categories II and III. Thus, the unstable and undefined elements of Categories II and III resulted in an incorrect decision by engineers, or in not achieving results even when a good decision had been made.

Before implementing CEDAC, we had often observed cases where a new production level led to an initial reduction in defects that was soon followed by a return to the original level. In addition to poor communication, other factors such as carelessness entered into play to cause defects as time passed. Even if some factor is originally part of Category I, there is no guarantee that it will remain there indefinitely. Continual communications and efforts are needed to maintain Category I. CEDAC assures this communication. The diagram is looked at by all persons concerned, and cards with new information are regularly placed over old ones each time an improvement is made.

Our method for transferring conditions in Categories II, III and IV to Category I could have important implications for fields other than quality control. In a communications/information-oriented society, where knowledge and information play a key role, effective methods for perfecting channels of communication will be at a premium. Management in this society will have to provide a system in which all employees concerned with a given problem share necessary information and voluntarily participate in achieving shared objectives.

3.10   DEFENSE (ADHERING TO ESTABLISHED STANDARDS) AND OFFENSE (FINDING NEW METHODS)

CEDAC had now spread throughout the company, and the number of diagrams which had been drawn by April, 1978 already exceeded 350. To test the hypothesis of the New Joharry's Window, eighty-six cases were randomly selected from twenty plants in ten divisions. The data from these eighty-six cases were analyzed quantitatively, then synthesized into a form easily understood by all employees. For employees to start practicing a new method, an understanding of that method based upon scientifically verified data is the most effective motivation.

The hypothesis of the New Joharry's Window implies two approaches to the solution of quality control problems:

- Devoting effort to Category I (adherence to established standards)
- Looking for new production methods in Category IV. Our

Our hypothesis is that the most productive route is to first work on transferring presently known methods and know-how to Category I; if the problem is still unsolved, then it is time to move into Category IV and look for new techniques.

Figure 3-8 classified the eighty-six cases into two groups:

(a) Groups which focused their efforts only on adhering to established standards.
(b) Groups which succeeded in finding new operation (production) methods;

The results shown here were tentative, and the possibility of achieving further results was not investigated.

The reduction of defects by group A was attributed to their adherence to previously formed methods. Their percentage of reduction is less than that of group B. Therefore, of the two approaches, it became clear to us that, for reducing defects, discovering new methods is more effective than just adhering to established standards.

An interesting conclusion can be obtained by further dividing group A into two sub-groups:

(a) Those groups which have always adhered closely to established standards;
(b) Those groups which did not and which still do not adhere closely to standards.

Figure 3-9 shows that even after new improved methods have been found, an important factor for the new methods' effectiveness is adherence by workers. Furthermore, it is also

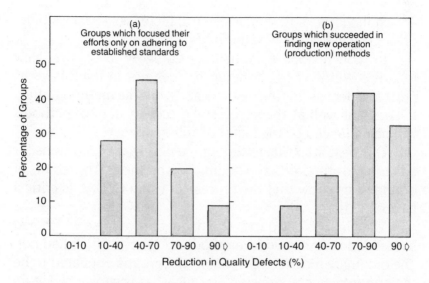

Figure 3-8 Finding New Methods versus Adhering to Established Standards

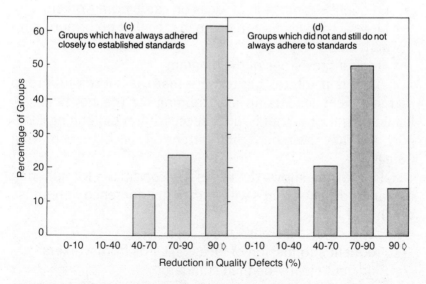

Figure 3-9 Groups Which Found Effective Methods as a Direct Result of CEDAC

shown in Figure 3-10 that adherence increases the possibility of success in finding new methods.

In conclusion, establishing Category I of the New Joharry's Window, i.e., adherence, does not in itself have as great an effect as finding new methods, but the methods' effectiveness, as well as the successful discovery of new methods, will be enhanced by the factor of adherence.

Our next step was to determine necessary conditions for adhering to standards and finding new methods. The results of our analysis show that the process of using CEDAC is critical to both of them.

The eighty-six groups were divided into those which had succeeded in finding new methods and those which had not. The distinguishing factor between the groups appeared to be their approaches to drawing up CEDAC as is shown by Figure 3-10. The successful groups were those which had:
- A high level of adherence to former standards
- Frequent submission of ideas on cards from workers
- More active discussion compared to that of former group activities
- Frequent revisions of the diagram

Also, is it interesting to note that the successful group had sufficient leadership and training for the newly established operations. That is, after successfully challenging Category IV, they switched their attention back to achieving Category I.

Figure 3-11 shows the necessary conditions for adhering to standards. The groups with sufficient adherence were those which had:
- Frequent discussions
- Frequent submission of ideas on cards from workers
- Sufficient clearly-defined standards
- Adequate worker participation in drawing up CEDAC itself

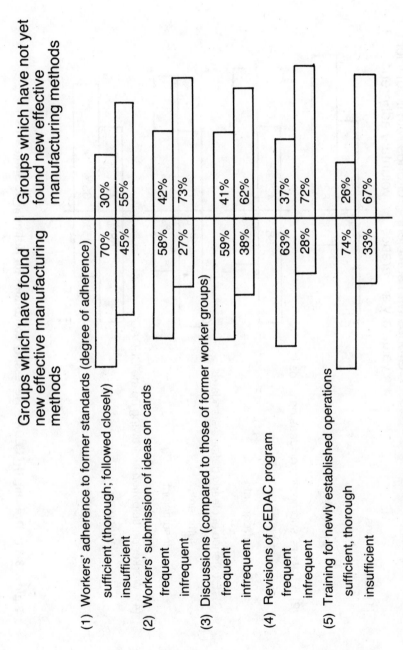

Figure 3-10 Drawing Up CEDAC: Adhering to Standards Gives Rise to New Methods

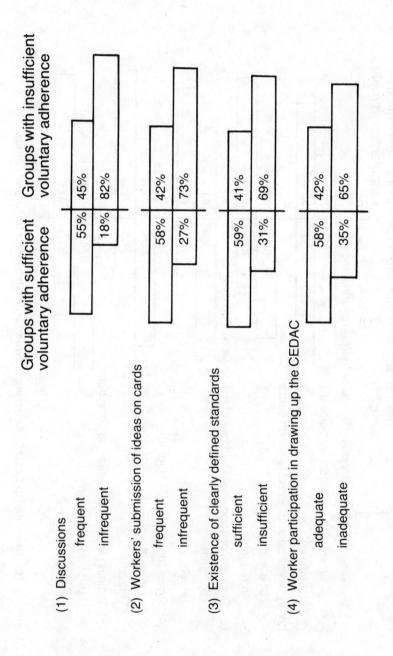

Figure 3-11 Drawing Up CEDAC: Necessary Conditions for Adhering to Standards

It should be noted that this information, drawn from actual experience, shows quantitatively how essential it is to have both the participation of all persons concerned and mutual trust among all of the group members in order to promote the adherence to standards and the constant development of improved methods.

3.11 CREATING A CEDAC MODEL

Next we developed a CEDAC model which can be used to forecast the results of ongoing CEDAC activities. Figure 3-12 shows the steps by which the model was formulated.

The CEDAC model has two objectives:
- Forecasting the possible outcome of ongoing CEDAC activities
- Helping us determine which factors should be controlled in order to obtain the most desirable result under any given conditions

Only part of the CEDAC model and our research results are described below. The entire study was detailed in *Hyojunka to Hinshitsukanri* (*Standardization and Quality Control*; August-September 1978, Japanese Standards Association). This paper was awarded the prize for best QC paper by the Deming Prize Committee in 1978. A summary was also carried in *Quality Progress*, the journal of the American Society for Quality Control.

A tool, if it is to be useful, must achieve tangible results. Figure 3-13 shows the percentage of losses due to quality defects against sales from 1976 to 1979. It decreased by approximately 50%. These results were not obtained exclusively through CEDAC, but rather through company-wide QC activities of which CEDAC was the backbone.

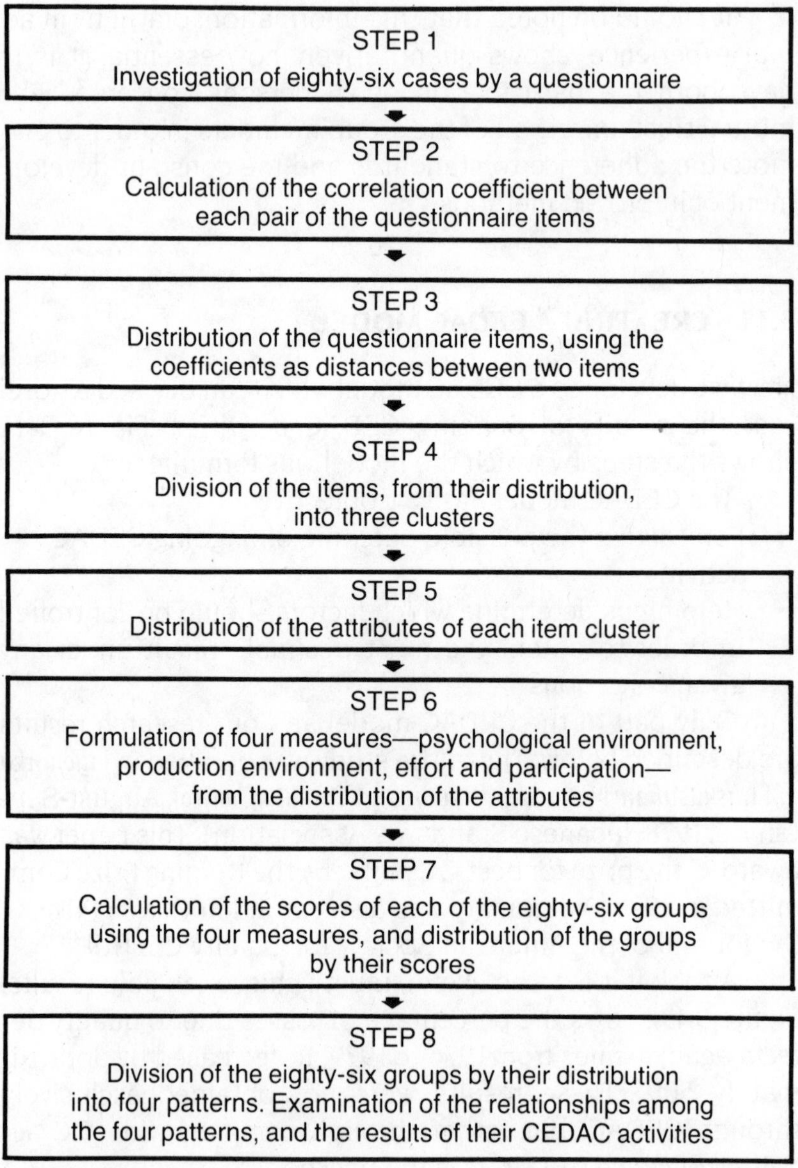

STEP 1

Investigation of eighty-six cases by a questionnaire

⬇

STEP 2

Calculation of the correlation coefficient between
each pair of the questionnaire items

⬇

STEP 3

Distribution of the questionnaire items, using the
coefficients as distances between two items

⬇

STEP 4

Division of the items, from their distribution,
into three clusters

⬇

STEP 5

Distribution of the attributes of each item cluster

⬇

STEP 6

Formulation of four measures—psychological environment,
production environment, effort and participation—
from the distribution of the attributes

⬇

STEP 7

Calculation of the scores of each of the eighty-six groups
using the four measures, and distribution of the groups
by their scores

⬇

STEP 8

Division of the eighty-six groups by their distribution
into four patterns. Examination of the relationships among
the four patterns, and the results of their CEDAC activities

Figure 3-12 Formulation of the CEDAC Model

3.12 GROUPING OF THE QUESTIONNAIRE ITEMS

Twenty-three items which influenced the results of CEDAC applications were selected. From the correlation coefficients of each pair of the twenty-three items it was found that these items fall into three groups:

(1) Items concerning the production environment such as defect frequency and the number of operations producing defects;

(2) Items related to the psychological environment, such as concern shown by managers and motivation for solving problems;

(3) Items regarding the use of CEDAC itself, such as revision of the diagram and submission of ideas on cards.

The degree of influence of each item was calculated in

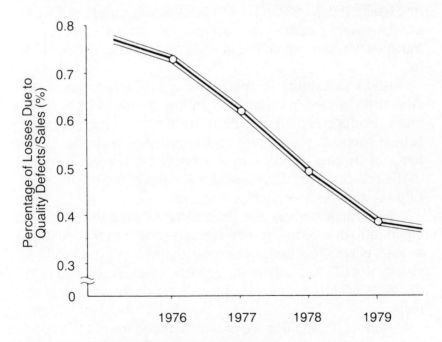

Figure 3-13   Decrease in Quality Defect Rate

Steps 5 and 6. Figure 3-14 shows the results of this calculation for items related to the production environment. Attributes with a more positive index have a more favorable influence on the production environment. Items characterized by a relatively large range between positive and negative attributes show a greater influence on the production environment.

We observed that the single most influential attribute is sufficient adherence to former standard, which again supports the hypothesis of the New Joharry's Window. Second in influence is management's commitment to emphasizing product quality rather than efficiency. The second item, defect rates, is significant, and shows that a lower frequency encourages more appropriate actions. This means that reducing the defect rate improves the production environment and facilitates further defect reduction. The timing of defect detection is also important. If defects can be spotted without delays and without hampering operations, solving QC problems becomes much easier. Devices enabling early detection are quite helpful.

Items pertaining to the psychological environment are similarly analyzed in Figure 3-15. Influential items include the group leader's experience, motivation for solving problems (which supports my contention that we should choose problems we are eager to solve in our own work), the leader's view of the reliability of CEDAC, workers' views of the reliability of CEDAC, and the concern of managers.

Regarding Item 3, it is interesting to note that a nearly equal ratio of veterans to new workers produces the least desirable effect. The items referring to leaders' and workers' views of CEDAC's reliability reflects their expectations of CEDAC's usefulness as a tool for dealing with serious problems.

Although the influence of Item 9, the range of CEDAC activity, is not in itself extremely significant, it does raise another important point. Suppose the overall probability of success for

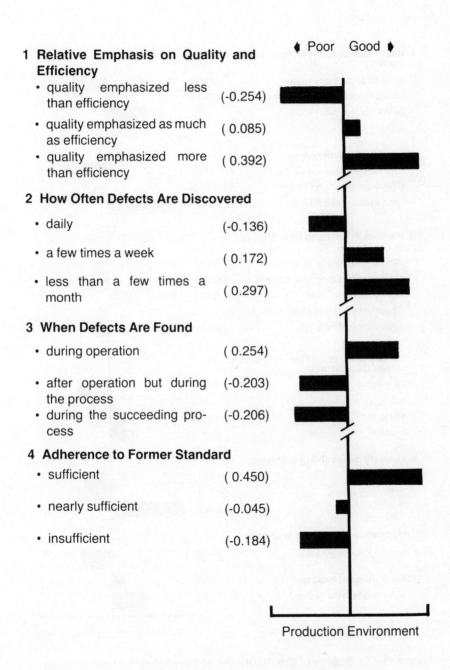

1 Relative Emphasis on Quality and Efficiency

- quality emphasized less than efficiency   (-0.254)
- quality emphasized as much as efficiency   (0.085)
- quality emphasized more than efficiency   (0.392)

2 How Often Defects Are Discovered

- daily   (-0.136)
- a few times a week   (0.172)
- less than a few times a month   (0.297)

3 When Defects Are Found

- during operation   (0.254)
- after operation but during the process   (-0.203)
- during the succeeding process   (-0.206)

4 Adherence to Former Standard

- sufficient   (0.450)
- nearly sufficient   (-0.045)
- insufficient   (-0.184)

◀ Poor   Good ▶

Production Environment

Figure 3-14 Scores of the Attributes of Production Environment

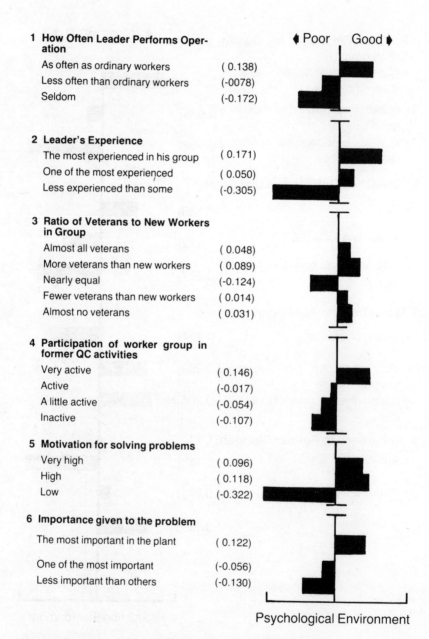

1 How Often Leader Performs Operation

As often as ordinary workers	(0.138)
Less often than ordinary workers	(-0078)
Seldom	(-0.172)

2 Leader's Experience

The most experienced in his group	(0.171)
One of the most experienced	(0.050)
Less experienced than some	(-0.305)

3 Ratio of Veterans to New Workers in Group

Almost all veterans	(0.048)
More veterans than new workers	(0.089)
Nearly equal	(-0.124)
Fewer veterans than new workers	(0.014)
Almost no veterans	(0.031)

4 Participation of worker group in former QC activities

Very active	(0.146)
Active	(-0.017)
A little active	(-0.054)
Inactive	(-0.107)

5 Motivation for solving problems

Very high	(0.096)
High	(0.118)
Low	(-0.322)

6 Importance given to the problem

The most important in the plant	(0.122)
One of the most important	(-0.056)
Less important than others	(-0.130)

◀ Poor   Good ▶

Psychological Environment

Figure 3-15 Scores of the Attributes of Psychological Environment

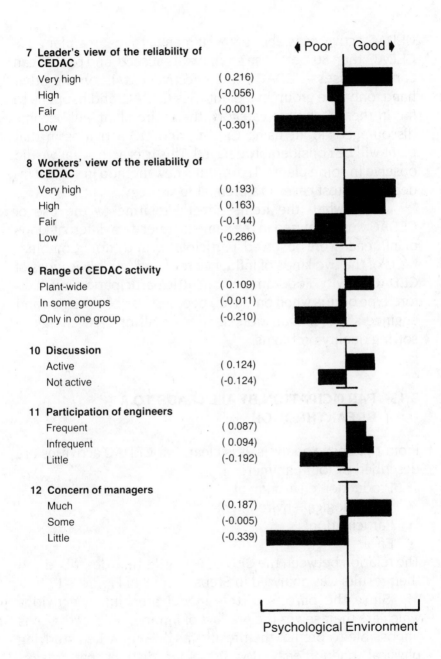

7 **Leader's view of the reliability of CEDAC**
Very high   (0.216)
High   (-0.056)
Fair   (-0.001)
Low   (-0.301)

8 **Workers' view of the reliability of CEDAC**
Very high   (0.193)
High   (0.163)
Fair   (-0.144)
Low   (-0.286)

9 **Range of CEDAC activity**
Plant-wide   (0.109)
In some groups   (-0.011)
Only in one group   (-0.210)

10 **Discussion**
Active   (0.124)
Not active   (-0.124)

11 **Participation of engineers**
Frequent   (0.087)
Infrequent   (0.094)
Little   (-0.192)

12 **Concern of managers**
Much   (0.187)
Some   (-0.005)
Little   (-0.339)

◀ Poor   Good ▶

Psychological Environment

CEDAC activities is about 80%. If many groups in a plant use CEDAC, then 80% of those groups will succeed, and people can correctly assess CEDAC's true effectiveness. If, on the other hand, only one group in a plant tries CEDAC, and happens to fall in the 20% failure category, the entire plant will become discouraged about using CEDAC, and QC activities in that plant will be considerably delayed. This is exactly what we did observe in some plants. Trying out a new method in several independent test cases is a preferable strategy.

Next, when the items directly relating to the use of CEDAC were analyzed in the same manner, two different kinds of influence were observed: participation and effort. Combinations of the two kinds of influence revealed four basic types of CEDAC activity. For example, the "little participation/much effort" type occurs when only a few people, possibly foremen and engineers rather than workers, devote all of their energy to solving quality problems.

3.13   PARTICIPATION BY ALL LEADS TO A BREAKTHROUGH

From the above analysis, it is clear that CEDAC activities are described by four parameters:
- Production environment
- Psychological environment
- Participation
- Effort

The relation between the CEDAC activities thus described and their results was analyzed in Steps 7 and 8 of Figure 3-12.

Since the objects of this model are human activities which are themselves the product of innumerable factors, it is impossible to predict their results as one can when studying physical phenomena. However, four distinct patterns of

CEDAC activities did appear. Furthermore, we analyzed how successful the groups of each pattern were in finding methods and in achieving adequate levels of adherence. As a result, it has become clear that the success of each group is closely correlated to the pattern to which it belongs. Table 3-3 gives a list of the characteristics of each pattern.

Pattern A. Benefiting from better environments, both participation and effort were high. The groups were successful in finding new methods and in achieving high levels of adherence. Results were very satisfactory. Almost all cases where speedy and considerable results were obtained fall exclusively into this pattern.

Pattern B. Both environments were poor, and not much extra time was left for problem-solving efforts. However, participation was sufficient. Discovering new methods was difficult for groups fitting into this pattern, but sufficient adherence was easily obtained. Fair results were derived as a result of this adherence.

Pattern C. Working in a fairly good environment, group members expended much effort in trying to solve their problems. They were often successful in finding new effective methods, but their adherence was not good, probably as a result of limited participation. The results were fair or considerable, but slow.

Pattern D. Both the production and psychological environments were poor. Neither participation nor effort was sufficient. The overall results were poor.

From all that has been mentioned above we have derived the following principles concerning CEDAC activities:

(1) Groups working in a good environment should aim at Pattern A. If, as is the case in Pattern C, only a handful of people work hard to find new methods, a longer period of time will be needed.

(2) Groups working in a poor environment should aim at

	Production Environment	Psychological Environment	Participation	Effort	Finding New Methods	Adherence to Standards	Results
A	□	□	□	□	□	□	● ⊗
B	×	×	□	×	×	□	○ ●
C	□	□	×	□	□	×	○ ⊗
D	×	×	×	×	×	×	◇ ○

□ = Good   × = Bad

Symbols of Results

	Percentage of reduction in quality defects		
Time period	0–40%	40%–70%	70% and above
Less than 3 months		●	⊗
3 months or more	◇	○	∅

Table 3-3 Patterns of CEDAC Activities: Where the Defect Rates Decreased

Pattern B, which emphasizes participation because these groups do not have extra time to spend on problem-solving efforts. Through active participation, these groups can improve environments so that they also can aim at Pattern A in the future. In other words, Pattern B is a breakthrough for a positive circle.

3.14 CONCLUSIONS FROM CEDAC APPLICATIONS

The results of the study made it clear that our work contains some important and unexpected implications for managerial engineering itself, and not just for the application of CEDAC.

The following are our key findings:

(1) It is generally accepted that a critical series of steps must be followed in the solution of quality control problems: analysis, improvement, standardization and adherence. In the above it has been proved that adherence is more than a means to achieve quick and significant results. It is also a springboard for developing quality improvement methods. Furthermore, it is a method for ensuring and increasing the effectiveness of newly discovered methods.

In other words, it is necessary to go full circle in Figure 3-16 from complete adherence to the manufacturing and operating standards which are already known. This must be repeated until the percentages of quality defects are reduced to satisfactory levels.

(2) It is sometimes felt that management is caught in a bind between participation, which is a slow process, and downright elimination of quality defects. The data we have obtained show that these two goals can be fully integrated. The participation of all persons concerned is indispensable in achieving complete adherence as well as finding new methods.

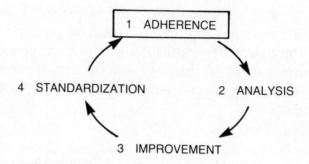

Figure 3-16   The Adherence-Improvement Cycle

It is wrong to eliminate participation on the grounds that it takes too much time. On the contrary, it is necessary in order to bring about solutions in a short period of time. This has been demonstrated in our efforts to solve quality control problems. As a final remark, it should be added that participation should always be directed towards a clear-cut, concrete objective.

An ancient Chinese thinker, Han Fei, wrote:

A king once asked a painter, "What are the most difficult things to draw?" The painter replied: "Dogs and horses." "Then what are the easiest?" asked the king. The painter's answer was "Monsters." It difficult to draw ordinary animals such as dogs and horses because everyone knows them and watches them every day, which means the painter cannot paint them carelessly. Monsters, on the other hand, are easy to draw because no one has actually seen them, and the painter can draw them any way he likes.

Since I began my career in the Research and Development Division, I have often said, half in jest, that it is more difficult to develop managerial engineering than to develop production engineering and other R&D. The objects of managerial engineering (quality, productivity, production control, etc.) are obvious to everyone. Even people in marketing and personnel divisions have something to say about them. Non-specialists always find it easier to talk about managerial engineering than about such technical subjects as R&D.

Painters of dogs and horses must exercise great skill if they hope to sell their works; drawing what everyone knows well is difficult. Fortunately for these painters, however, they may actually and easily observe their subjects. If they observe carefully, they note fantastic lines and colors. Having actual objects to draw is a great source of strength for this kind of painter. Similarly, detailed and analytical observation is the first step in managerial engineering.

3.15 QC FOR THE CONSTANT PRODUCTION OF HIGH QUALITY PRODUCTS

The study of CEDAC sheds light on a critical point, for the implementation of quality control. We must achieve a state where manufacturing and operating standards are known and practiced by everyone. QC activities provide the means by which we may achieve this state and thus secure ever higher levels of product quality (Table 3-4).

	Through Equipment...	Through Personnel...
Cause	i) Keep a high level of uniformity by controlling all equipment through careful, complete maintenance.	ii) Achieve and maintain the situation in which the best standards of manufacturing (operation) methods are correctly practiced by all workers.
Effect	iii) Detect abnormalities in the quality of final products and in-process materials by continuous mechanical measurements. Take immediate corrective actions towards the subnormal process and goods. (Adjustment of causes, process control, segregation and repairs of defects.)	iv) Detect abnormalities in quality by using quality checkers or operator-inspectors. Take immediate corrective actions towards the subnormal process and goods.

Table 3-4 How QC Activities Lead to Quality Improvement

They include functions not only for maintaining standard conditions, but for restoring them and eliminating defects when deviations occur.

Table 3-4 was developed by analyzing and synthesizing fifteen actual cases where defects were drastically decreased by achieving complete adherence to existing standards. A veteran foreman once said: "Every item on this table represents exactly what we have been working hard for. Our daily efforts are directed towards realizing these four items." It is no wonder that defects are tremendously decreased when any one item on this table is realized.

In Table 3-4, item (i) refers to any part of the equipment that may influence product quality. If product quality is presently at a satisfactory level, then the state of every part of the equipment should be maintained as is. This means keeping a high level of uniformity through thorough maintenance. With regard to the part of the process which involves human workers, item (ii) aims at achieving a state where effective standard operations are known and correctly practiced by every worker.

3.16 THOROUGH PRACTICE

One of Sumitomo Electric's plants has been able to completely implement items (i) and (ii). As a result, perfect production quality has been the rule since March, 1976. Perfect production quality has been defined at Sumitomo as a state where no quality defect appears in any of the total processes of a plant. The plant in question achieved this perfect result through complete equipment maintenance and thorough training of workers.

The Quality Control Problem Study Group investigated how perfect production quality was achieved at this plant. The possible factors were listed on 400 cards which are summarized in Table 3-5. This book does not attempt to give the full details of the study, but rather to suggest to the reader that zero-defect production system was realized by reliable methods developed within the plant itself.

It should be noted here that there is a critical factor for developing reliable methods. This is the power to thoroughly practice reliable methods. Dr. Juran once said: "I have recommended quality control in the U.S. and in other countries, but it was only Japan that practiced my idea immediately." Managerial engineering can succeed only when reliable methods are reinforced through constant practice.

3.17 QUALITY COST

Our approaches to perfect production quality were introduced by the plant manager. His emphasis on education and training was evident: there were times when man-hours spent on off-the-job training reached almost 7 to 8% of total man-hours. The concept of quality cost was first expressed in *Total Quality Control* by Armand V. Feigenbaum (McGraw-Hill, New York, third edition 1983). It is a standard used for managerial decision making and the resolution of quality control problems. "Quality cost" is defined as the ratio of total costs spent for quality control to sales, including prevention costs (QC education, etc.), appraisal costs (inspection and experiments, etc.) and failure costs (losses due to defects and claims, etc.). In terms of this concept, a plant without defects may not be maximizing its profits. I don't think that every plant should approach perfect production quality. Still, the concept of perfect production quality is helpful. It points out a desirable direction and leads to a competitive advantage that cannot otherwise be readily realized. Plant A's quality cost data are shown in Table 3-6.

The Quality Control Study Group attacked the problem of quality costs head-on by challenging the widespread tendency

1. Maintenance of work environment.
- Keep floors and equipment clean.
- Keep everything in order.
- Train operators to repair equipment by themselves.
- Keep a low noise level. (Slowing down motors may be necessary.)
- Check and maintain pass lines and detectors.

2. Consistency in fundamentals. •
- Be punctual.
- Do physical exercise and running.
- Be a reliable person and develop trustworthy relationships with others.
- Encourage foremen to take initiative.

3. Inspection of equipment.
- Maintain equipment at peak condition. (Do not overlook even a loose screw.)
- Organize the inspection patrol, which consists of the plant manager, foremen, and leaders of worker groups.
- Promptly follow the advice of the inspection patrol.
- Let the plant manager take the initiative in inspection patrol.
- Make inspection in all areas, i.e., safety, quality, and productivity.

4. Elimination of dangerous operations.
- Make safety top priority.
- Warn each other by writing safety memos and safety ratings.
- Organize the safety committee and encourage it to patrol.
- Utilize warning memos and safety campaigns.
- Utilize safety ideas of workers and develop failproof and foolproof systems. (Standards should be easy to adhere to.)

5. Quality assurance in each process.
- Be responsible for the goods you process.
- Let process checkers be responsible for in-process quality control.
- Prevent the recurrence of defects.
- Utilize automatic detectors effectively.
- Send defective goods back and help those responsible to understand the cause of the defect.
- Eliminate all defects in a pilot production.
- Take economical measures to solve defects.
- Let workers experience the benefits of statistical methods rather than dwell on the minute details of the methods.
- Impress workers with the importance of quality.

6. Complete personnel training and information exchange.
- Train new workers one-to-one, on the job. Teach them how to do it, let them do it, and evaluate their work. Train new employees until they can respond well to accidents.

- Use spare time for study meetings.
- Use morning meetings and other opportunities to exchange necessary information.
- Encourage workers to learn by themselves, and to experience the delight of successful improvement.
- Put emphasis on the process of workers' improvements rather than their results.
- Evaluate workers with multi-dimensional measures, and group workers with complementary abilities and characters together.

7. Paper tests for workers.
- Practice safety tests, prepared by the group leaders.
- Practice standard tests to encourage workers to learn operation standards. (Standards are improved through these tests.)

8. Operations standards.
- Establish practice standards.
- Describe key points and know-how clearly so that each worker can follow them easily.
- Put cards which visually show key points and know-how on all equipment.

9. Immediate detection and complete elimination of equipment failures.
- Establish preventive measures for equipment failures through the examination of maintenance records and with the cooperation of the equipment designing staff.
- Stop machines if there is any possibility of failure. (Operators themselves should ask the help of maintenance workers.)
- Organize an operators' equipment course to teach them about the mechanics of the equipment.

10. Emphasis on systematic preventive maintenance.
- Emphasize preventive maintenance.
- Systematize maintenance operations, and then improve their efficiency.
- Use a shock pulse meter to predict bearing deterioration.
- Use the card system for inspection of equipment. (The man-hours needed for maintenance operation should be managed by this system.)

11. Leaders of worker groups active as frontline managers.
- Assign targets to each group and check the results (targets such as amount of cost reduction, work efficiency, failure and repair cost, loss rate, attendance rate, amount of overtime work, and number of safety improvement ideas).

Table 3-5 Realizing a Zero-Defect Production System: A Summary of

- Let group leaders report on their group results at a performance review meeting in the plant. (The results should also be reported within the groups.)
- Through the cooperation of groups, aim at high performance for the entire plant.
- Encourage group leaders to participate, starting from the initial planning stage.
- Assign each group leader a task concerning the entire plant, and encourage him to follow up on that task. (Possible tasks are quality, production engineering problems, training, improvement ideas, safety, work environment, productivity, equipment, and materials.)
- Organize group leaders through the division of tasks, and provide a back up staff system.
- Improve the quality of group leaders through the measures mentioned above, until, for instance, they can talk to the accounting staff knowledgeably.

12. Respect for the creativity of the line people (foremen, group leaders, and workers.)
- Provide as many opportunities as possible for the line to think by themselves.
- Rely on the line's creativity.
- Assign a part of the staff's task to the line.
- Provide an environment in which every person can develop his ability and no one is left behind.
- Encourage the staff to back up the line.
- Encourage workers to make direct contact with the plant manager in case of emergency.
- Utilize all the opportunities, such as company-wide study groups, to encourage improvement.
- Utilize meetings to get new ideas from the line. (Do not criticize poor results, but with the line, analyze why they could not achieve good results.)
- Put emphasis on wise investments for cost reduction, rather than on small savings.
- Aim for high performance and high motivation through rationalizations, which is carried out with respect to all workers.

13. Day-to-day management with the participation of all persons concerned.
- Encourage all (including workers) to participate in management and control.
- Estimate every day's performance through day-to-day management.
- Enthusiastically use the ideas of younger workers.
- Emphasize creative use of spare time rather than the rigid "efficiency-first" principle.
- Organize work divisions and group divisions effectively.

14. Use of interchange training to broaden skill development.
- Establish a flexible manpower allocation system to meet the variable production level.
- Broaden and improve every worker's skill.
- Expand interchange training to include maintenance workers and inspectors.
- Record every worker's skill using the skill table which describes the operations he can perform and evaluate the level of his ability.
- Encourage workers to participate in interchange training.
- Use interchange training for teaching workers how to operate the crane and the forklift.

15. Continual, steady improvement.
- Improve quality and efficiency. Reduce loss, scrap materials and the number of operators.
- Improve equipment. Use brand-new equipment efficiently. Fully utilize the equipment's designed capacity.
- Establish a computer system that can be used by workers.
- Encourage workers to make value analysis ideas and change design specification if needed.

16. Utilize an idea system for steady improvement.
- Let group leaders quantitatively estimate the results of the workers' ideas. Teach them calculation methods for estimating the results.
- Utilize the idea bank and idea note.

17. Perfect quality production achieved through the enthusiasm of all, and maintained in a relaxed atmosphere.
- Work to achieve perfect quality production first in the process with the most difficult problems. (Success here will increase the enthusiasm of all persons.)
- Maintain perfect quality production in a relaxed atmosphere.
- Try to solve the biggest problems first. (Success here leaves much time for further problem solving.)
- Define the measures for effectiveness of maintenance operation.

18. Definition of perfect quality production and recognition, by all, of the achieved results.
- Define perfect quality production, including the problems which bring big losses, and the problems which involve everyone.
- Publicly share successful achievements (for example, by giving special badges and marks on helmets, taking commemorative photographs, and planting commemorative trees).
- Utilize the award system for improvement ideas, safety ideas, special tasks, training, etc.
- Be patient while working toward perfect quality production.

the QC Problems Study Group's Ideas

Period Cost Items	1974 (2nd half)	1975 (Ave.)	1977 (Ave.)
Prevention (%)	35	44	62
Evaluation (%)	42	47	37
Failure (%)	23	9	1
Quality Cost (as a % of total sales)	6.7	2.6	1.7

Table 3-6 Quality Cost Data for Plant A

to tackle only failure costs (on the assumption that prevention costs and appraisal costs are fixed). The concept of quality cost is not widely practiced in Japan, probably because of the difficulties companies encounter in obtaining accurate data. But we should not worry about this too much as long as the concept remains usable. Defining a clear rule of calculation is sufficient for offsetting minor inaccuracies. Known prevention, appraisal and failure costs on quality provide us with a common measure. The data also provide important information by which we can examine the waste in each cost and set a cost-down target.

Where managerial measurements are concerned, sensitivity to change is more important than accuracy. Even the first observation does not accurately express the absolute value of an object; its relative changes can be grasped by comparing the following observations with the first one. As long as such an observation suffices for our objectives, we should not hesitate to use it. By taking into account its defects, we can avoid misusing it.

We found certain cases in which the quality cost concept was particularly important. In some divisions, such as that which produces large electric systems, a product failure might result in enormous claims from the user. In such cases it is important to calculate potential failure costs from claims and accordingly set desirable levels for prevention and appraisal costs. We should take into account both actual failure costs which have been incurred, and possible ones, no matter how improbable they may appear. Prevention and appraisal costs should be budgeted on the basis of this calculation. Thus the concept of quality cost leads to strategic quality control.

The second space shuttle was launched into space in November, 1981. The mission was deemed a success. I have heard it said that its cost per pound was equal to that of platinum. Considering the actual manufacturing costs, prevention and appraisal costs must have been enormous, which reflects a huge amount of potential failure cost. It is significant that this potential failure cost had to include many intangibles, such as a potential loss of national prestige, in the event of a disaster.

3.18   A PROFESSOR FROM DENMARK

A professor of mathematics interested in CEDAC visited us in the fall of 1980. His name was Dr. Dahlgaard. When I explained the New Joharry's Window to him, he exclaimed: "Is it possible for us not to practice what we know? I do not understand the *known-unpracticed* category at all." He spent two days on this question. At the beginning, we were also puzzled by the mathematician's viewpoint on CEDAC. However, at the end of his study, he grasped the essentials of CEDAC. He wrote to us that he would give a lecture on CEDAC in Copenhagen in January, 1982.

While Dr. Dahlgaard was staying with us, one of our CEDAC groups achieved an astonishing result which is shown in Figure 3-17. Even in an automated plant, workers can make

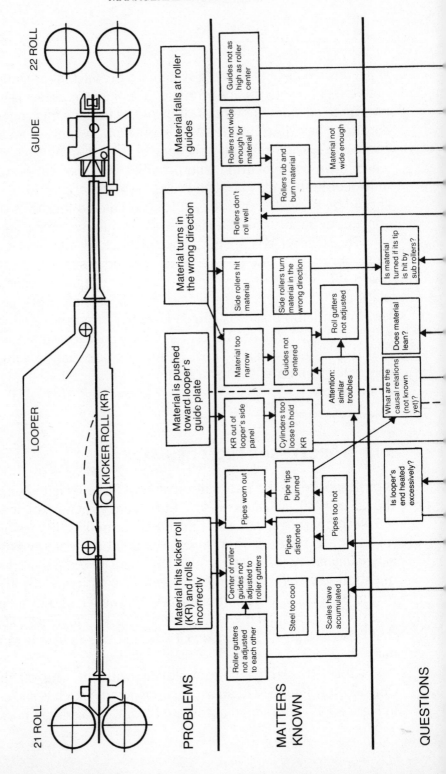

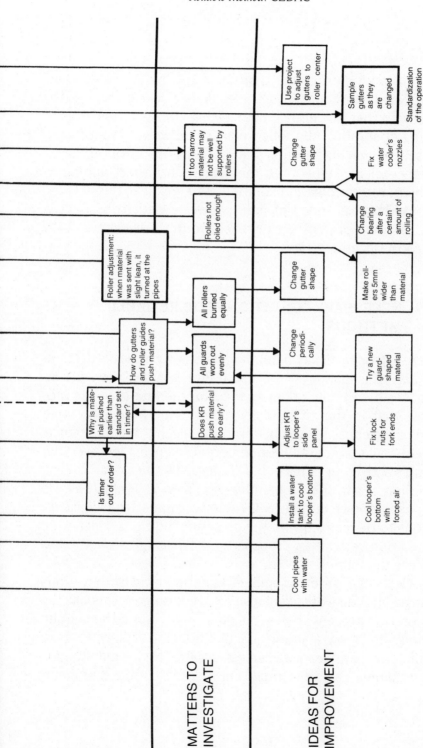

Figure 3-17 Workers List Problems Causing Defects in Rolled Steel Wire Operation — A CEDAC Approach

a significant contribution to problem solving. A CEDAC chart had been drawn to decrease the frequency of incorrectly rolled steel wire that was appearing between stands 21 and 22 in a rolling operation. "Mis-rolls" refers to defects in this process caused by machine troubles and operations errors. This experience clearly illustrated the process from fact-finding to problem recognition and solution. As a result of this activity, the productivity index of man-hours needed to produce a given amount of steel wire increased from 100 in October 1977 to 164 in December 1980.

3.19   NECESSARY CONDITIONS FOR RELIABLE METHODS

Figure 3-18 is taken, with minor revisions, from *How to Get Creative Ideas* (Hassoho, 1977), in which Professor Jiro Kawakita introduces his KJ (QC circle) method for the first time. He proposes that in the analysis of scientific methodology, three kinds of sciences should be taken into account: field science, speculative science, and experimental science. I reviewed our group's activity in terms of his W-shaped framework.

First of all, the problem was defined at Point A as the proposals shown in Table 3-1. There I compared the ideal conditions to be realized with the present conditions which were to be improved. I then proposed our own original method to achieve the former.

Next, the group members experimented with various changes in their work to achieve ideal conditions. This was the exploration process shown in Figure 3-18. I asked them, quite literally, to "grow a young plant." Choosing a plant to grow within one's own work was an essential factor for maintaining the members' zeal; it is important to keep in mind that members' energies should always be focused on solving their own critical problems.

The members brought their plants to the group meetings and exchanged ideas. This was observation B-C at the experience level. In this process, CEDAC was created by modifying cause-and-effect diagrams and control charts.

As CEDAC spread throughout the company, many remarkable results appeared (Table 3-2). The study group was excited and decided to investigate their causes. The hypothesis of New Joharry's Window was formulated; this was point D.

In order to explain the hypothesis, eighty-six cases of CEDAC applications were collected and analyzed (see Steps E, F and G). In the observation process from F to G, the computer

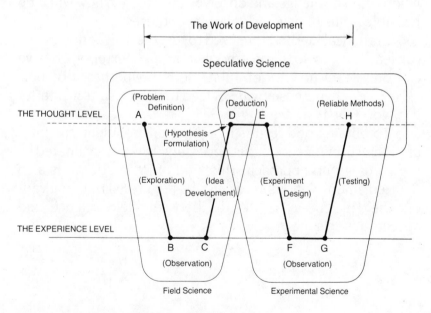

Figure 3-18 Scientific Methodology

and statistical methods were used to deal with many factors and an enormous amount of data.

At point H, the hypothesis was tested and valuable QC know-how was obtained. We did not forcibly work with this W-shaped framework in our minds. However, it does perfectly describe the process of our study. Knowledge and know-how obtained through these steps can be referred to as "reliable methods." The study group developed "theories out of practice" by adhering to these steps of scientific methodology.

It should be emphasized here that the quality of any hypothesis depends both on speculative science and field science. We must be simultaneously practical and theoretical in our outlook. Rather than trade off these two attitudes, we must integrate both. This is the reason that we must study theory and improve the quality of our observations at the same time. If both our knowledge and observation are poor, how will it be possible for us to develop sound hypotheses?

Statistical methods are used to test these hypotheses. We can learn how to do this in school or through textbooks, but we can only learn how to formulate sound hypotheses by ourselves. Poor hypotheses will not lead to solid results no matter how good the tests are.

To obtain good results in a plant environment, the integration of everyone's ideas is necessary. This was facilitated by the study group approach. This kind of integration was also realized among various study groups (Figure 8-1), among various field sciences, as well as between field science and speculative science.

Chapter 4

A RELIABLE METHOD (2): STOCKLESS PRODUCTION

4.1 PRODUCTION CONTROL — BASICS FOR THE MANUFACTURER

In industrial plants, production is carried out according to production plans. Establishing these plans is a basic daily task for the manufacturer. The goal is for materials to flow smoothly through processes until the final product is produced with designed quality.

In practice, production control is aimed at several objectives:

- To minimize the total man-hours needed for processing, or, in other words, to maximize output per man-hour
- To minimize total delivery delay
  (Most plants try to realize these first two objectives simultaneously)
- To minimize total production costs
- To minimize total work-in-process time

Does your plant prepare production plans with any of the above objectives in mind? Aiming at all of them at once is theoretically impossible, and it is the workers who are caught in the vise. Plants must establish standards in order to balance out these conflicting objectives, or to achieve one of these goals at the sacrifice of others.

The techniques of Operations Research (OR) enable plants to achieve any one of the four above-mentioned goals. Unfortunately, these techniques are impractical, because the size of the problems they can handle is too limited in scope (several jobs and several machines at most) compared to the actual problems faced even in a small plant which might comprise more than a thousand jobs and machines. However, understanding these relatively simple cases is indispensable for grasping the essence of the problem, and herein lies the true value of operations research.

Problem size and other factors make it difficult to apply the techniques of operations research in actual situations. Another factor is the need to know how the optimum solution will be affected by changes in the environment, something that is not easily determined by simple OR models. Furthermore, there are many cases where it is necessary to achieve several objectives simultaneously.

4.2 DEVELOPING THEORIES OUT OF PRACTICE

On October 25, 1944, the carriers of the U.S. Navy Task Force 51 were suddenly attacked by kamikaze fighters near the Philippines. The Navy had been continuously harassed by them for the last ten months of the war. Recognizing the seriousness of the problem, a conference was held at San Francisco from November 24-26, 1944. Several defense organizations participated in this conference and analyzed together all the available materials and possible countermeasures. A group of operations research specialists was also involved.

By analyzing how the fighters attacked and how American ships responded, the operations research group was able to find a solution for decreasing the rate of successful attacks. This solution was recommended to the Navy. Some ships adopted it, but others did not. Thus the solution was unintentionally tested during actual battles. Those ships that had adopted these tactics decreased the hit rate by 50%.

I hesitate to cite this serious case, but it demonstrates the effectiveness of operations research. The methodology for developing managerial engineering techniques, i.e., "developing theories out of practice," can be observed in this case. Or, rather, the methodology is operations research itself. Whether the objective be quality or productivity, this inductive method for developing managerial engineering can in fact be called OR.

As we said in Section 4.1, OR models are often too limited and simplistic to solve practical problems. But my understanding is that OR constitutes an attempt to simplify and model a complex phenomenon so as to clarify its essential structure. By constructing a clear (and often mathematical) model, we are able to deepen our understanding of the phenomenon. The model's role is not to describe every detail, but rather to provide a better basis for decision-making.

As an example of a mathematical model, consider the following which is used as a decision rule to establish the maximum electricity allowance (an explanation of the variables is omitted):

$$\frac{\dfrac{W_1}{\sum a_1}}{\dfrac{W_0}{\sum a_0}} > 1.1$$

$$W = W_1 \cdot \frac{\left\{ B_1 + 0.9(B_2 - B_1) + 0.7\left(\dfrac{\sum b}{D} - B_2 \right) \right\} D}{\sum a_1} \cdot \beta$$

How would it be possible to describe such a complex rule without recourse to mathematics? In the business world today, we are becoming accustomed to using similar mathematical models rather than redundant verbal expressions.

Through the use of these principles, we decided to start with an understanding of the structure and functions of the complex phenomenon (industrial production) to develop effective production control systems. We learned this approach of starting with a basic understanding of the system from some European firms visited in the summer of 1977. The writings of a famous Japanese IE researcher, Mr. Shigeo Shingo, were also quite suggestive.

4.3 MOVING TOWARDS STOCKLESS PRODUCTION

At the time we were beginning our efforts, Toyota's kanban system was rapidly spreading throughout Japan. My intention was to transform kanban into an engineering approach that could be practiced by anyone in any plant. With this end in mind, the Production Planning and Control Study Group was formed in October 1977. We also started an IE Applications Study Group with volunteers from other companies. The principles of stockless production were developed from the practice and study of these two groups. Strictly speaking, it should be called "less-stock" production, but this does not sound as good as the term "stockless."

Stockless production is a method for organizing operations that aims for maximum efficiency. This means producing necessary products in necessary quantities exactly at the time they are needed. It emphasizes the critical role of stock, or work-in-process, and attempts to develop planning and control systems for smooth material flow. It also helps realize this goal by suggesting improvements in production systems.

The greatest obstacle to obtaining ideal production conditions is learning how to approach the vastly complex problem of inefficiency. The stockless concept provides a key to this approach.

We shall use the term *process* to refer to materials flow; the transformation of materials by man or machine is termed *oper-*

ation. If plant management attempts to achieve both rapid materials flow from the perspective of process and minimize idle work-time from the point of view of operations, a conflict will arise.

The only way to resolve this conflict is to constantly implement improvements in the production system. The following data show that these two different objectives of process and operation can be made compatible by improvements. Figure 4-1 illustrates the percentages of stock reduction that have been obtained in stockless production applications in different types of manufacturing companies. Work-in-process was reduced by 48% on the average. As a result, manufacturing lead time was also reduced as shown in Figure 4-2. Productivity improvements simultaneously achieved in these cases are also shown in Figure 4-3.

The point is to make the contradictory objectives of process and operation compatible. The key parameter of this problem is the allowable stock between two consecutive steps in the production process. The term "stockless" was derived from this idea.

"Allowable" refers to the maximum stock at any point in the process. In general, of course, this is only the upper limit; constant effort is exerted to keep stock levels as low as possible. By controlling stock quantity, the characteristics of a stockless (just-in-time) production system are determined. Management sets this allowable quantity — zero, or a three-day supply, or whatever — taking into account how quickly improvements can be made.

Setting the allowable quantity too high does not make sense since the very existence of excess stock levels tends to disguise production problems. It is only when the plant is constrained to work with minimal stock levels that inefficient aspects of the production process leap to the surface, for all to see — and correct. If, on the other hand, the level of allowable

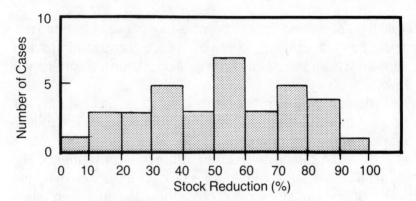

Figure 4-1 Work-In-Process Reduction

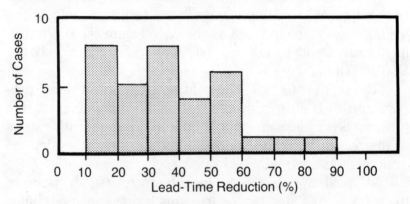

Figure 4-2 Manufacturing Lead Time Reduction

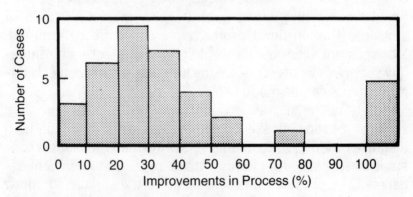

Figure 4-3 Productivity Improvement

quantities is set too low, necessary improvements cannot catch up with the overwhelming number of problems that crop up. This inevitably leads to workers secretly exceeding the allowance. In such a situation, improvements are actually delayed, contrary to management's intention.

4.4 PRODUCTION STANDARDS AS MANAGEMENT POLICY

Management should express its policy in terms of standards such as standard flow time and standard stock quantity. These standards need not be very sophisticated, but they must be rational. If production standards are to be respected by workers they must be practical and understandable. This is one of the most important lessons we learned from our experiences.

Although a detailed discussion of stockless production is not the objective of this book, some explanation of standard flow time and standard stock quantity is in order.

Standards for Planning and Control

(1) *What are standards?*
Standards are used to control material flow between consecutive steps in the production process, and thus to control the total flow in a plant. Starting from the production deadlines, material flow between any two consecutive steps is controlled from downstream to upstream, smoothing the total flow.

The basic task of production control is to determine what, when and how much to make. To do this, material flow must be controlled through either of two dimensions: time or quantity.

A standard established in terms of time is called "standard flow time." It is the time required for material to go through two consecutive steps [Figure 4-4(a)]. In most cases it is determined for each machine, taking into account lot

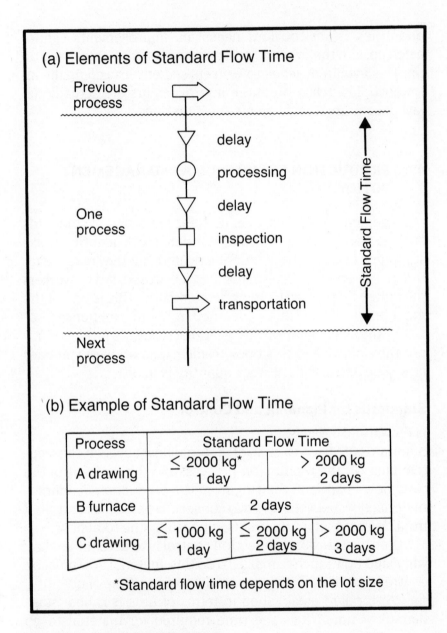

Figure 4-4 Standard Flow Time

sizes. Quantity refers to production speed and is expressed in terms of production quantity measured in units per day. It is termed "standard production quantity."

(2) *The role of standards*
Standards serve for control as well as planning:
- By comparing changing production conditions with standards, each process can be understood in terms of what should or should not be done at each moment.
- As workers try to adhere to standards, problems in the production process are detected. They are swiftly recognized and solved by all of the persons concerned.

Therefore, standards serve as the basis for control and improvement. In plants where only a limited variety of products are manufactured, material flow can be grasped in terms of visible stock quantity instead of flow time. The standard stock quantity is determined as follows:

Standard Stock Quantity =
Standard Production Quantity × Standard Flow Time

The two systems using standard flow time and standard stock quantity are compared in Table 4-1. In fact, many plants do not measure materials in terms of stock quantities. Plants producing a great variety of products fall into this category. This type of plant cannot introduce Toyota's kanban system which uses stock quantity to establish standards. But if flow time is used for standards instead of quantity, the same kind of control is possible. Stockless production is therefore possible in any kind of plant.

Standard flow time or stock quantities determine the characteristics of a production system. Using these standards as control parameters, one can develop an actual production system. Detailed rules are secondary problems; one can set

System	Standard flow time system	Standard work-in-process quantity system
Applicable to:	Make-to-order	Make-to-stock
Standard	Standard flow time is determined from manufacturing man-hours and allowable delay. Divisions of standard flow time should be within the span of control of foremen and workers. Starting date of each process is determined by the delivery date and standard flow time.	Standard work-in-process quantity is determined by the capacity of a process and the demand fluctuation of the subsequent process. Standard work-in-process quantity is often used instead of standard flow time, because work-in-process quantity can be visually controlled.
Control method	Production schedule for each order is planned by the use of standard flow time.	Production order is placed to keep work-in-process quantity at a fixed level.

Symbols

▷ : Flow of material

→ : Flow of information

Control card prepared for each order accompanies the material.

Control card prepared for each product shuttles between two processes.

table of standard flow time

Process / Product	A	B	
	days		
P₁	3	1	...
P₂	②	③	...

table of standard work-in-process

Process / Product	A–B	B–C	
	pieces		
H₁	40	10	...
H₂	㉛	30	...

Table 4-1 A Comparison of Two Control Systems

them at will. It may not be easy, but this is not critical as long as rational standards reflecting management policy are set.

4.5 THE CHARACTERISTIC APPROACH

It is important for those who practice managerial engineering to have a clear idea of what they are doing. If a method develops out of a clear understanding of basic facts, it will lead to significant productivity improvement. The lack of understanding is often a cause of failure when a method is blindly applied.

As the work of the Production Planning and Control Study Group proceeded, stockless production was applied in many plants of Sumitomo Electric and its affiliated companies. Several other firms reported that the production stock quantities were significantly reduced by following stockless production procedures.

In July 1978, just a year after the start of the Production Planning and Control Study Group, the IE Applications Study Group was formed at the Kansai Institute of Management and Information Sciences with fifteen volunteers from other firms and universities. I was appointed chief of this group. This was an excellent opportunity to gather information on stockless applications in other companies. The group was run on the idea that the basic principles of stockless production can be applied in any type of plant, in spite of the fact that actual methods will vary from one application to another.

4.6 EBB TIDE AT THE SEASHORE

Figure 4-5 shows the relationship between stock levels and various production problems. When the stock level is high, it covers production problems just as a high tide covers reefs.

[With large work-in-process quantity]

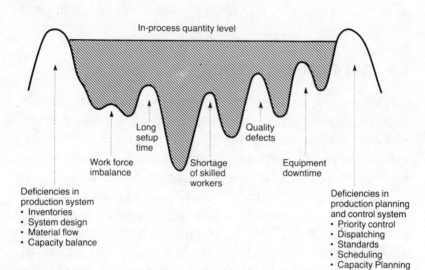

[With small work-in-process quantity]

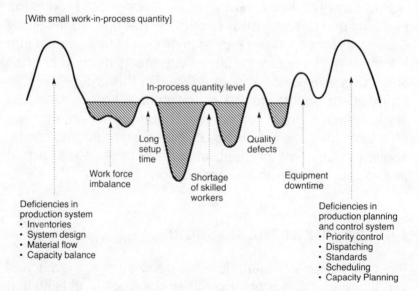

Figure 4-5   Work-In-Process and Production Problems

When production stock levels decrease, production problems crop up like reefs appearing one after another at low tide. If one has sufficient will to make improvements, stock level reductions can become a powerful technique for detecting and solving problems.

There is a problem wherever production stock accumulates. Reasons for this accumulation are summarized in Table 4-2. The seven reasons given in the table interact with each other, and thus increase production stock in many cases.

There are other cases where no clear reasons are detected. For example, if a shop operates one shift a day, while the downstream shop operates on two shifts, work-in-process for one shift will suffice. There are many cases however, where three or four days worth of stock is accumulated. In the testing or packaging process, it is often observed that a handful of workers are swamped with work-in-process. In such cases,

Reasons for WIP Accumulation	Identifiable Problems
1. Not obvious	1. The appropriate level of WIP is not determined
2. Imbalance in capacity (including difference in shifts)	2. Capacity is not balanced between processes
3. Lot sizes too large	3. Set-up operations take a long time
4. Too many independent shops each with WIP	4. Extreme division of labor was made with consideration to productivity only
5. Frequent defects and machine downs	5. Quality control and equipment maintenance are insufficient
6. Absence of skilled workers	6. Workers' training is insufficient
7. Production done too early	7. Production control system is ineffective

Table 4-2 Reasons for Work-In-Process Accumulation

there may be no valid reasons for piled up stocks. But even in these cases, there are real problems that cause work-in-process accumulation. Stockless production does not hide these problems under high levels of work-in-process. It tackles them by using low stock levels to bring them to the surface.

4.7 BUILDING A BASIC MODEL

I introduced my ideas on OR models at the beginning of this chapter. Because of these ideas, we wanted a basic model that would enable us to understand complex phenomena of production control and to develop a control system based on this knowledge. It is desirable for such a model to be used for experiments that will produce visible facts rather than abstract knowledge because only facts obtained through experience can generate new ideas when we are confronted with new phenomena. The thirteen principles enumerated in Table 4-3 were developed as a model to serve this purpose.

Principles 1 to 6 were obtained from simulations created by the Japan Management Association and first described by Mr. Shigeo Shingo in one of his books.

Let me briefly introduce the simulation.

Simulation Rules
- Figure 4-6 is the form used in the simulation — the arithmetic tool should be used as specified for each problem
- Eight people perform this simulation
- People are referred to as *workers*, arithmetic tools as *equipment*, and calculation as *operation*
- Items I-IV are referred to as *products* — one sheet of paper contains four products
- Eight sheets are used in the simulation — therefore, the total number of products to be made is thirty-two
- By inserting a different number in the parentheses of each

Principle 1
There are two dimensions of production, which cross each other: "process" and "operation."

Principle 2
Delay occurs as the result of division of labor, and transportation occurs when a process is divided into subprocesses.

Principle 3
There are two kinds of delays: "lot delay" and "process delay." (Lot delay refers to the delay of one item while other items of the same lot are processed. Process delay occurs when a whole lot waits between processes.)

Principle 4
The greater part of manufacturing lead time consists of delays.

Principle 5
Process delay is considerably reduced by balancing the line and diminishing bottlenecks.

Principle 6
Lot delay is reduced by the division of lots.

Principle 7
Limiting in-process material to smaller quantity is an effective means for shortening manufacturing lead-time.

Principle 8
Balancing the line is effective in shortening of manufacturing lead time and, at the same time, in raising efficiency.

Principle 9
Whether a line is well-balanced or not, efficiency plunges to a much lower level if in-process material is totally eliminated (i.e., no delays). Thus, the optimal number of in-process units should be determined deliberately in order to balance efficiency and lead time.

Principle 10
Capacity should be immediately adjusted to the fluctuation of load in order not to increase lead-time (or process delay).

Principle 11
Waiting time before production begins should be adjusted by controlling backlog.

Principle 12
Shortening the planning cycle leads to the reduction of waiting time.

Principle 13
Maintenance of stock of semi-finished products is an effective means to shorten manufacturing lead time of made-to-order products. However, the stock should be kept at a minimum.

Table 4-3 Principles for Production Control

ITEM I

a	b	c	d	e	f	g
①	M	3 + 4 + 2 + 9				
②	M	① x 6 + 8				
③	A	② + 145 + ① + 212 - 176				
④	W	③ x 6 ÷ 15				
⑤	A	④ + ③ + ② - 240 + ①				
⑥	M	⑤ x 2				
⑦	M	⑥ ÷ 4				
⑧	S	⑥ x ⑦ + 25				

ITEM III

a	b	c	d	e	f	g
①	M	7 + 12 + 25 + ( )				
②	M	① x 2 - 10				
③	A	① + ② + 425 + 182 - 504				
④	W	③ ÷ 2 x 13				
⑤	A	④ + ① + ② + 85 + ③				
⑥	M	⑤ x 4				
⑦	M	⑥ ÷ 6				
⑧	S	⑦ x ⑥ ÷ 120				

ITEM II

a	b	c	d	e	f	g
①	M	17 + ( ) + 6 + 11 + 21				
②	M	① ÷ 4 + 8				
③	A	250 + ② - 175 + ① - 43				
④	W	③ x 12 ÷ 7				
⑤	A	① + ② + ③ + 160 - ④				
⑥	M	⑤ ÷ 3				
⑦	M	⑥ x 8				
⑧	S	⑦ ÷ 13 x ⑥				

ITEM IV

a	b	c	d	e	f	g
①	M	( ) + 12 + 29 + 7 + 12				
②	M	(① - 20) x 2				
③	A	① + 811 + 98 - ② + 153				
④	W	(③ - 759) x 3				
⑤	A	115 + ④ + 318 - ② - ③				
⑥	M	⑤ ÷ 7				
⑦	M	⑥ x 3				
⑧	S	⑦ ÷ 17 x ⑥				

Legend:
- a = Process
- b = Method
  - M = Memory arithmetic
  - A = Abacus
  - W = Calculation with figures written down on paper
  - S = Slide rule
- c = Problem
- d = Answer
- e = Starting time
- f = Ending time
- g = Total time for each problem

Figure 4-6　Simulation Form

paper, we can change the arithmetic problem
- Processes ① through ⑧ should be carried out in order.
- Numbers ① through ⑦ in each problem indicate that the results of previous calculation should be used accordingly.

Simulation Outlines

The following five simulations are conducted in order.

Simulation 1: Before Division of Labor

Operators ◊

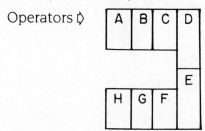

- Each of eight operators calculates the entire problem on one sheet of paper.
- Each person works in the following order: Item I, Processes ① through ⑧ ; Item II, Processes ① through ⑧ ; and so on through Item IV, Process ⑧

Simulation 2: After Division of Labor (Lot Production)

Processes ◊

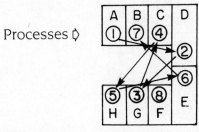

- Processes ① through ⑧ in the chart above indicate the assigned work to each operator.
- When each operator completes his part of the calculation on one sheet of paper, he hands the paper to the next operator. For example, Operator A calculates in his head each Problem 1 of Items I through IV on the first sheet.

Then he gives it to Operator D, who works on each Problem 2. Operator A starts calculating each Problem 1 on the second sheet. This procedure simulates the lot production with the lot size of four.

Simulation 3: With Consideration of Workers' Skill and Work Flow (Lot Production)

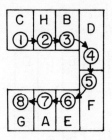

- The division of labor is arranged according to workers' skill.
- The layout of processes is arranged according to work flow.
- Each operator works on four assigned problems (lot) at a time, as described in Simulation 2.

Simulation 4: After Division of Lot

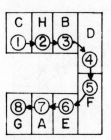

- Cut each sheet of paper into four pieces along the broken lines indicated in Figure 4-6.
- The assigned operation to each worker and the process layout are in the same manner as in Simulation 3.
- Now, each operator has one problem on each paper. After

completing his work, the operator hands the paper to the next person.

Simulation 5: After Line Balancing

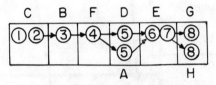

- The main purpose of this layout is synchronization of each process. Therefore, in assigning work to each worker, the consideration of his skill is confined to a certain extent.
- The processes and the operators are rearranged based on work load.

The simulation results are shown in Figure 4-7.

Computer simulations were used to obtain Principles 7 through 9 of Table 4-3. As Principle 4 states, the greatest part of manufacturing lead time consists of accumulated delays, and avoiding unnecessary work-in-process leads to significant reductions in total lead time. From this knowledge, the following simulations were conducted to analyze how limits to work-in-process affect production in terms both of the process objective (speed) and the operations objective (quantity).

Figure 4-8 shows the results of these simulations. Work-in-process is limited to specific quantities, as shown on the horizontal axis. In Case 1, the production line is well balanced, with each process having a cycle of fifty minutes and a fluctuation of plus or minus two minutes. Although the production line in Case 2 has the same cycle time, it is not well balanced; fluctuation is as great as forty minutes.

The vertical axis of the left panel shows the process objective, average manufacturing lead time, and the vertical axis of the right panel (operations objective) namely, average efficiency.

SIMULATIONS

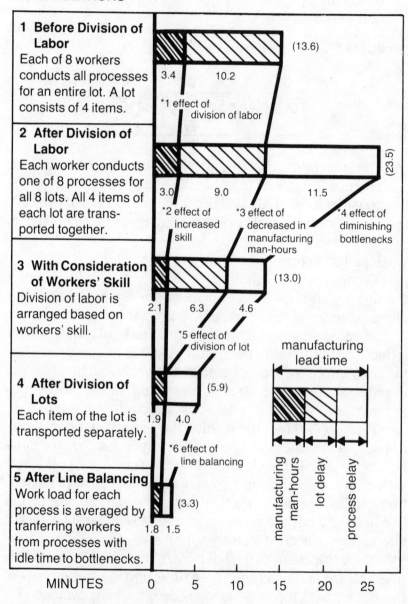

1 Before Division of Labor
Each of 8 workers conducts all processes for an entire lot. A lot consists of 4 items.

(13.6)

3.4   10.2

*1 effect of division of labor

2 After Division of Labor
Each worker conducts one of 8 processes for all 8 lots. All 4 items of each lot are transported together.

(23.5)

3.0   9.0   11.5

*2 effect of increased skill

*3 effect of decreased in manufacturing man-hours

*4 effect of diminishing bottlenecks

3 With Consideration of Workers' Skill
Division of labor is arranged based on workers' skill.

(13.0)

2.1   6.3   4.6

*5 effect of division of lot

4 After Division of Lots
Each item of the lot is transported separately.

(5.9)

1.9   4.0

*6 effect of line balancing

5 After Line Balancing
Work load for each process is averaged by tranferring workers from processes with idle time to bottlenecks.

(3.3)

1.8 1.5

manufacturing lead time

manufacturing man-hours

lot delay

process delay

MINUTES   0   5   10   15   20   25

Figure 4-7 **Manufacturing Man-Hours and Lead Time**

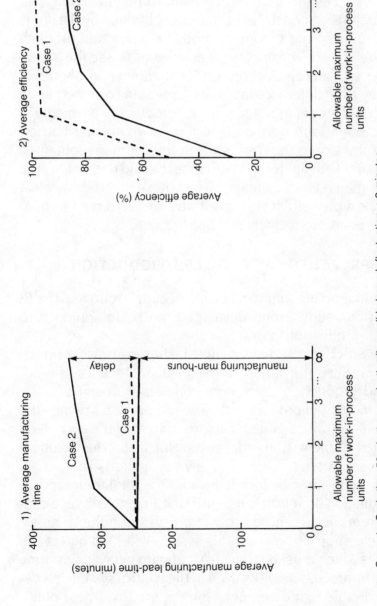

Case 1: Cycle time 50 minutes; production line well-balanced; fluctuation ± 2 minutes.
Case 2: Cycle time 50 minutes; production line unbalanced; fluctuation approximately 40 minutes.

Figure 4-8 Results of Limiting Work-In-Process Material

The remaining principles were obtained from the study of the balance between load and capacity using input/output charts as well as the analysis of manufacturing lead time.

The thirteen principles in Table 4-3 obtained by the study group produced our model for production control. Although the model may be incomplete, it enables us to see the essential aspects of any production control phenomenon. There will always be a big difference in results, depending on whether we have a basic model or not for solving production problems.

Although I am not happy to remind you of war battles, please think about the results which the OR model obtained against kamikaze fighters. Those ships that did not employ the model suffered twice as many hits as those that did. This fact should be a powerful lesson to all who are concerned with increasing plant productivity and product quality.

4.8 APPROACHES TO STOCKLESS PRODUCTION

The Production Planning and Control Study Group and the IE Application Study Group developed the basic approach to stockless production, as follows.

(1) Stockless production must be based upon the principles of production control. Although characteristics of products and production differ from company to company, the basic principles of production and work-in-process remain the same. First of all, it is necessary to understand the thirteen principles (Table 4-3) in order to develop a stockless production system suited to each company's characteristics.

(2) Delay must be avoided within the total framework of the production system. It is essential to think in terms of a control system for the entire production system rather than for any single shop or process. This system will help detect the problems which must be solved. A standard delay in flow time or work-in-process quantity used in the control system is a decision variable that determines the required swiftness of im-

provements. Such a control system clearly shows the priority of production problems to everyone concerned. When this goal is established for everyone, timely and swift improvements in productivity are achieved.

(3) Improvements in the QC and IE activities, the production system, and the production control system must be pursued simultaneously. To obtain stockless production, improvements to remove obstructing problems as well as effective production and production control systems for the smooth flow of materials are essential. Stockless production is impossible without these three factors (see Figure 4-9).

(4) The target level of stockless production must be determined by management of the production division. The process objective is given first priority. Nonetheless, the operation objective must also be kept in mind, and various improvements, such as set-up time reduction, equipment maintenance, and quality control must be made accordingly. Therefore, the target level and approach speed of stockless production must be determined with due consideration for the plant's ability to make the necessary improvements. Management of the production division must show firm determination and a clear conception of its ability to achieve these goals.

(5) Production control through total participation must be pursued. Stockless production cannot be achieved by the planning and control division alone. All the workers must perceive the system of materials flow and understand what they are expected to do. In other words, everyone controls and monitors his own work in stockless production. It is important for all the workers to share necessary information and decide what they should do at each step. Control systems that provide visual information are very effective for this purpose. By production control through total participation, stockless production aims at avoiding old-fashioned systems with shortage lists and expeditors.

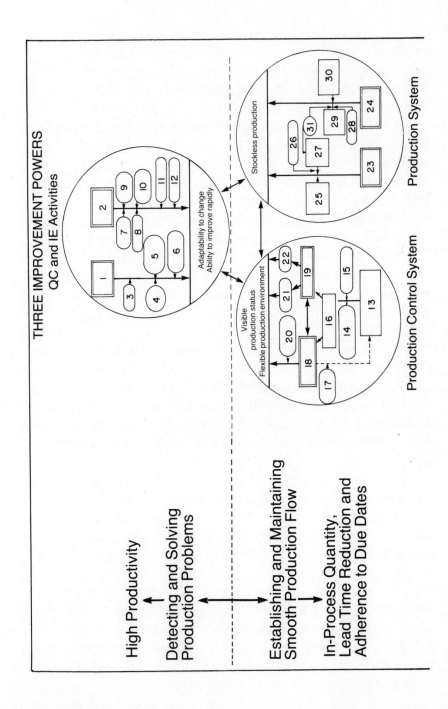

Key:

1. Allocation of flexible workforce
2. Improvements in product quality and equipment
3. Multi-skilled workers
4. Skill improvement
5. Establishment of standard operations
6. Formation of improvement groups
7. Foolproof devices
8. Shortened setup time
9. Automatic machine suspension
10. Pre-automation
11. CEDAC
12. Perfect quality production
13. Flexible scheduling
14. Shortened planning cycle
15. Non-periodic planning
16. Use of standards

17. Visual control systems
18. Order-backlog control
19. Lead time control
20. Control of standards
21. Direct control of material flow
22. Control boards
23. Speedy production flow
24. Semi-finished goods inventory
25. Production line differentiation by product group
26. Integration of production steps
27. Leveled production flow
28. Shortened setup time
29. Small lot production
30. Workload leveling at planning stage
31. One piece flow

Figure 4-9   Relationship Among Methods for Achieving Stockless Production

4.9　HOW STOCKLESS PRODUCTION WAS DEVELOPED

There was a basic task to be realized by the manufacturing firm: achieving smooth production flow. Improvements in this area had long been desired, yet it was still a new frontier for IE and OR in our company. Some of the managers in charge of production control were involved in this task and longed for even the slightest payoff from their work. They had valuable expertise gleaned from their vast experience.

Existing IE and OR methods were quite limited in their potential practical applications. However, they did provide us with a basic model for production control, and stimulated our thinking. Although these factors were nothing new, we did anticipate integrating them in a new way. The Production Planning and Control Study Group and the IE Application Study Group provided the opportunity for this new integration.

First order law:　Law of duel or strategy for the weak

$$m_o - m = e \times (n_o - n)$$

m_o : enemy's initial workforce
m　: enemy's remaining workforce
n_o : our initial workforce
n　: our remaining workforce
e　: exchange rate (or weapon efficiency)

Second order law:　law of concentration effect or strategy for the strong

$$m_o^2 - m^2 = e \times (n_o^2 - n^2)$$

Table 4-4　Lanchester's Law

New combinations of existing knowledge are an important means for reaching new horizons in engineering. For instance, a survey of seventeen newly developed American weapon systems was conducted, which reported that 95% of the basic techniques utilized in these systems had been developed forty to fifty years ago. Furthermore, four of the six most innovative systems were nothing but combinations of existing techniques.

A great desire to achieve improvements is indispensable. We realized that it was essential for everyone concerned to do his best in order to reach the highest levels of creative problem solving.

4.10 SECOND THOUGHTS ON OR

It is widely believed that OR is more effective for prevention than for actual treatment. The law shown in Table 4-4 was formulated by Philip Morse and George Kimball in their famous book *Methods of Operations Research* (MIT Press & J. Wiley, New York, 1951). The first order law is called the "law of duel" or, from another viewpoint, "strategy for the weak." Here, n_0 and n represent our workforce before and after a battle. Therefore, $n_0 - n$ shows our losses in the battle. Similarly m_0, m and $m_0 - m$ are the enemy's initial workforce, remaining workforce and losses.

If this model is applied to our work, $m_0 - m$ is the remaining workload to be done, and $n_0 - n$ shows consumed resources to be consumed, such as manpower, costs and material. Let e stand for the exchange rate which compares the effectiveness of weapons or workforce between the two parts. If $e = 1$, the initial workforce difference remains unchanged after the battle.

I would like to talk about e for a moment. In our study groups we tried to improve its value. The "reliable methods" and "practice by all" which we discussed at the beginning of this book are means for raising the value of the exchange rate, e. This exchange rate may be used to relate past and present, or us and a rival company.

The characteristics necessary for managerial engineering to become a reliable tool are: (1) It must be applicable by anyone, anywhere, at any time; and (2) it must be so suitable for us that we are able to use it with total confidence. The latter is not meant to imply compromise with our present situation. Simply, the engineering methods must improve our creativity, coincide with our management culture, and aim at long-term improvements.

As I have stated again and again, both (1) and (2) above suggest that the creative use of this original knowledge is indispensable to the successful application of managerial engineering. Copying from other firms always creates weakness. This point is also important for integration. Successful integration with the ideas of others must be based on one's own strengths.

Regarding "practice by all," it was not the insufficient level of our own knowledge that obstructed our effective application of managerial engineering. It was our practice that was insufficient. A strong sports team must practice abundantly in addition to possessing great skill. That which we are unable to obtain quickly may represent a true competitive advantage. Managerial engineering obtained through abundant practice can become a source of tremendous strength.

When five units of a red army and four units of a white army fight each other with an exchange rate of one (in, say, a medieval war), the white army is completely destroyed, and one unit of the red army survives. In a modern battle, the number of remaining units[2] equals $5^2 - 4^2$. Thus, the red army will be left with three units rather than one after the battle. I actually experienced the principle behind this kind of exchange in the guise of workload (enemy workforce) versus design manpower (our workforce) while building a new plant. A plant had to be constructed by my division on a new site, and I was in charge of the project. It was the first time we had attempted such a project, and we were very inexperienced. We decided that since we were using inexperienced people, we would use a larger workforce — more manpower — than was actually required.

At that time, the division had three other plants, and available plant engineers for the project were drawn from all three of them. The project's workload fluctuated, as it proceeded, from five to three to six. As a result of our policy, we were able to bring the plant to successful completion in spite of our lack of experience. Needless to say, the plant managers alone were not the only reason for our success; many people inside and outside of the division gave their entire support.

In spite of the fact that the project was a success, I would have been able to do it with less manpower if I had known Lanchester's law — the law governing the exchange between the red and white armies. I should always have employed one more unit of manpower than was required.

The reader may doubt how it is possible to quantify the workload as just described. I reply that it is the manager's (not the computer's) responsibility to assimilate and control such unquantifiable factors.

If you make it a rule to use four units of manpower for five units of workload, you should reconsider your policy. Unless your exchange rate is truly extraordinary, your "armies" risk defeat on every front. The Prussian Army's basic strategy, for instance, was to concentrate all the workforce as swiftly as possible in order to destroy the best forces of the enemy. On account of this strategy, railroads were more important to them than fortresses.

I recommend that the reader use OR models informally in his daily work. It is always easy to find someone who has a good knowledge of OR and who can provide many constructive suggestions. There is no need for using formal OR terminology. Fruitful thinking is more important. We can not achieve anything until a problem is first thought out.

The leader must be able to spot scenarios for success by integrating what he needs to maximize $e(n_0 - n)$. That is, he must find and show his subordinates a strategy for winning, or, at least, not losing.

The higher the leader's position, the more important this task becomes. Nothing is more irresponsible than for the leader to put his subordinates on the front without any prospect of victory. The leader should develop his scenario for success and take the lead by showing it to his subordinates. Needless to say, mere hard work is not enough for him.

I introduced my idea on motivation in Chapter 2, when discussing the hydrogen accident prevention project. There are numerous books on motivation now, but I believe the true means of motivation lie in the leader's communicating a scenario for success which can be accepted and believed by all his subordinates. All other means of motivation do little more than offset negative factors.

Furthermore, I have learned that the most effective means for everyone to accept and believe an idea is understanding based upon scientific discovery.

In general, managers do not use OR very effectively. If they just make the effort to implement its basic principles, they will be rewarded by increased productivity. Both rational thought and unexpected inspiration are necessary conditions for creative work. When one pursues rational thought by building an OR model, he may very well be led down unexpected paths. Such unexpected paths lead to creativity.

Chapter 5

A RELIABLE METHOD (3): IE IMPROVEMENTS

5.1 ROBOTS AND IE

New technologies such as robotics, automation and the increased electronic sophistication of machinery are changing the world of industry. Industrial engineers especially cannot afford to neglect progress in this field.

The other day I watched a publicity film by a robot manufacturer. I was astounded to observe several times in the film that his robots performed useless motions. I thought they were funny and felt a sort of affection for these almost-human robots. I learned, at the same time, that the efficiency of a robot depends on whether or not its designers are familiar with the principles of motion study in the field of IE.

In June 1976, six months after we had started the Quality Control Problem Study Group, we started the Motion and Time Study Group. Its tasks were to develop:
*   Management by standard time
*   Principles and techniques for operations improvements
*   Skill analysis

Although the objects of study were different, the basic principles for the study group were the same as those for the Quality Control Problem Study Group.

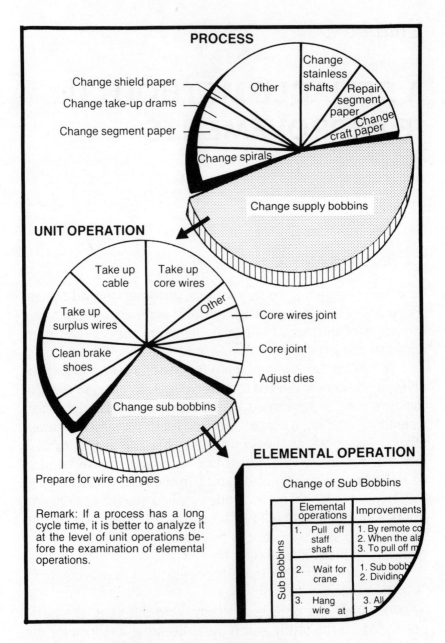

PROCESS

Change shield paper

Change take-up drams

Change segment paper

Other

Change stainless shafts

Repair segment paper

Change craft paper

Change spirals

Change supply bobbins

UNIT OPERATION

Take up cable

Take up core wires

Take up surplus wires

Other

Core wires joint

Clean brake shoes

Core joint

Adjust dies

Change sub bobbins

Prepare for wire changes

Remark: If a process has a long cycle time, it is better to analyze it at the level of unit operations before the examination of elemental operations.

ELEMENTAL OPERATION

Change of Sub Bobbins

	Elemental operations	Improvements
Sub Bobbins	1. Pull off staff shaft	1. By remote co 2. When the ala 3. To pull off m
	2. Wait for crane	1. Sub bobb 2. Dividing
	3. Hang wire at	3. All 1.

Figure 5-1　An Example of Operation Analysis

5.2 REDUCING SETUP TIME

At this time we were behind other firms in the reduction of setup time. Therefore, as a background for our research, we visited several firms that are successful in this field. They very graciously spent time with us and discussed the problems they had encountered and the results they had achieved. We often heard: "We even worked on Saturdays and Sundays," or: "The manager never went home before 11 P.M. during that time."

Although each case seemed different from others, we found a common factor in these successful cases. It was nothing but the analytical approach suggested by IE's forefathers, about seventy years ago. We adopted this approach to their problem of setup time reduction with a single modification that all concerned employees participate, rather than an isolated handful of industrial engineers.

More specifically, this approach suggests that operations be divided into their basic elements, as is seen in Figure 5-1. The importance of each of these elements is then weighed. The basic steps for setup time reduction as developed by the Motion and Time Study Group are shown in Table 5-1. We compiled this approach from various successful cases in other companies by analyzing them according to the perspective of traditional IE.

5.3 THE "BUNT" STRATEGY

At the "idea generation" step in Table 5-1, it is always possible to find an alternative idea which achieves 70 to 80% of the effects at 10% of the original idea's cost. Engineering staffs tend to conceive of ideas which may achieve impressive results, but at an excessive cost. Making large investments also requires a lot of time for decision-making. A plant that has only this kind

STEP	DESCRIPTION
Choosing a setup operation	Set the objective clearly. 　e.g. shorten the setup time by 80% for: 　　small lot production 　　reducing operators 　　expanding production capacity Choose an operation which greatly needs improvement. 　e.g. operations which: 　　take a lot of time 　　are very tiring 　　involve difficult adjustments 　　are very frequent Choose a specific machine rather than a group of machines.
Observation and measurement	Measure average mean time in typical case. (A small number of cases will suffice.) 　e.g. cases of major products 　　cases of products with frequent production Apply time study for short cycle operation. Apply operation analysis at one minute intervals for long cycle operation, making description at level of elemental operation. Measure operations with higher frequencies at a more detailed level.
Summing up	Prepare a summary form and fill it out. Post it where it will attract suggestions from many people.
Analysis	Examine the purpose of each elementary operation and possible results if it is abolished. Examine from as many viewpoints as possible. Use cards—they are effective in attracting and presenting many people's ideas without requiring meetings.

Table 5-1　Basic Steps for Setup Time Reduction

STEP	DESCRIPTION
Idea generation	While examining purposes, try to improve operations that: require a tiring posture require physical strength are unpleasant to perform interrupt the rhythm of work require attention Hold meetings to gather ideas. Generate as many ideas as possible which can be realized quickly and cheaply even if their effects are limited. Utilize hints for reducing setup time: (1) Draw a clear line between internal setup (done while a machine is stopped) and external setup (done while a machine is working). (2) Change internal setup to external setup. (3) Apply one-touch fixing and removing. (4) Eliminate adjustments. Develop alternative ideas with 80% effectiveness and 10% cost.

	Effects	Costs
Original idea	1	1
Alternatives	0.7 ~ 0.8	0.1

STEP	DESCRIPTION
Execution	Try the new ideas, easiest ones first. Have manager and engineers examine effects of new ideas on product quality and safety.
Maintenance	Measure the result of the improvement using day-to-day management. New ideas may be obtained in this process. Standardize the new operation after it is stabilized, to maintain the achieved result.
Repetition	At appropriate intervals, repeat the above steps.

of improvement project characterized by long lead times will generally be subject to low morale among those employees who are most concerned by those improvements.

There is a surer way than this "home run" strategy: that is, scoring by a series of hits and bunts. Starting in December 1977, six months after the beginning of the setup time reduction project, the Motion and Time Study Group began to obtain the results shown in Table 5-2. The data were gathered four times, each showing about 40% of the average rate of reduction. Figure 5-2 illustrates distributions of the reduction rates. It should be noted that the proportion of projects with rates of 70% or more remained constant throughout the three investigations. The data show that by following the basic steps 30% of the projects will achieve reduction rates of 70% or more. The study group achieved its initial objective, that is, the development of a reliable method that can be used by anyone, anywhere, to realize the expected results.

Table 5-3 gives an example of setup time reduction. The change of dies that used to take sixty-one minutes and fifty-five seconds now takes seven minutes and five seconds. The number of nuts and bolts used was drastically reduced from fifty-eight to eleven, and tools, from five to one.

Our approach to setup time reduction was a slight modifi-

	December 1977	March 1978	August 1978	December 1978
Number of projects completed	121	186	278	308
Average rate of reduction in setup time	40.0%	38.5%	41.5%	40.5%

Table 5-2   Shortening of Internal Setups (Done While the Machines Are Stopped)

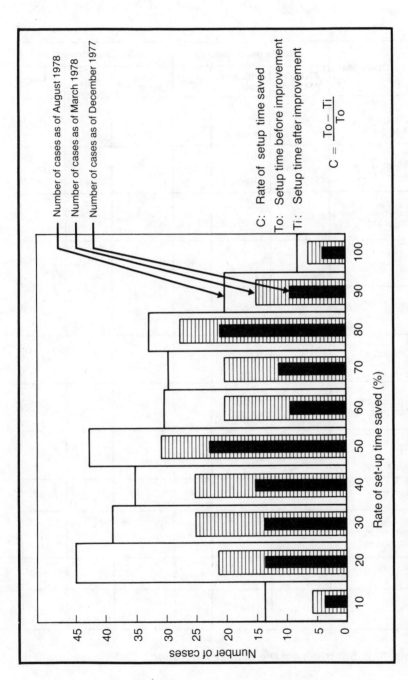

Figure 5-2 Cases as Classified by the Amount of Time Saved

Unit Operation	Before improvement			After improvement		
	Fixing Method	Bolts, Nuts, Tools	Time	Fixing Method	Bolts, Nuts, Tools	Time
Set a stand for the upper pounder	bolts	M10 bolts ×6 air wrench	1'15"	bolts	M10 bolts × 3 air wrench	40"
Set an upper pounder	fixing board bolts	M8 bolts ×2 air wrench	40"	one-touch fixing		02"
Set an adjust-ing board	M8 nuts	M8 nuts ×12 monkey wrench	12'30"	one-touch fixing		02"
Set a die	fixing board bolts	M10 bolts ×6 air wrench	3'50"	a split die nuts	M27 nuts × 4	2'00"
Set a support	nuts	M27 nuts ×4 air wrench	1'50"			
Set a knife shaft	fixing board bolts	M6 bolts ×16 air wrench	8'40"	one-touch fixing		08"
Set and adjust a center plug	screw	monkey scale	3'50"	one-touch fixing		02"
Set a fork shaft	springs a hoist	— —	6'20"	one-touch fixing		15"
Subtotal			38'55"			3'09"
Others (in-cluding addi-tional work)		M27 bolts ×12	23'00"	a turntable shelves for tools	M27 bolts × 4	4'41"
		42 bolts			7 bolts	
Total		16 nuts	61'55"		4 nuts	7'50"

Table 5-3 Shortening a Die Change Operation

cation of the basic IE approach. This modification included microscopic examination of an operation and idea generation by all the people who were concerned. It enabled us to:

- Easily eliminate purposeless motion
- Save improvement costs
- Obtain many new ideas
- Try these ideas quickly

Before the development of this approach, I had once asked a plant engineer how he was proceeding (in terms of Table 5-3). He answered: "Reducing the die setup time is our main project. We have tried three ideas with considerable results in the past three years. Now we've got another plan, but it will cost fifteen million yen, so we are trying to get budget approval. We hope to complete the plan in ten months."

The difference between the costs and speed of these improvement projects is staggering.

I remember a meeting where a three-year, long-range plan was being discussed. Actually, there was little discussion. But when the meeting was over and the topic of the layout of the bicycle parking lots came up, people suddenly began to talk with animation. Someone remarked that it was a pity that the discussion of the long-range plan had not been so lively.

Rather than be sorry, it would make more sense to break down the discussion of the long-range plan to the level of "parking lots" and think about that problem in very basic terms. If we only look at problems at the macro level, our situation appears unchanged over the past couple of years. The same people discuss the same problems over and over, such as weaknesses in quality control, subsidiary management, etc.

However, if we look at problems at a more detailed level, we find many differences between today and three years ago. We must be able to perceive such differences in our situational and problem analysis. I will discuss the analysis of situations in Chapter 7.

5.4 IMPROVING MAIN OPERATIONS

Returning to the setup time reduction projects, let me introduce another important lesson we learned through our experiences. Improving setup operations is nothing but improving
main operations; what we obtained in setup time reductions
can be applied to the improvement of main operations themselves.

Formerly, the most common goals of industrial engineers, such as the minimization of idle time or the optimiza-
tion of layout, material handling, etc, did not always involve
the improvement of main operations. It was not without cause
that workers often complained that their jobs became harder
after improvements.

Our approach to reducing setup time eliminates wasteful
and purposeless elements in main operations, and enables
the worker to do his job with much less time and effort. Thus it
comes as no surprise that our approach gained the full and enthusiastic support of workers.

In a previous chapter I spoke of the evidence we possess
for actual work improvements. We obtained this skill through
experimentation in many projects and through observing hun-
dreds of cases. Anyone can apply this approach if he has
sufficient opportunity to experiment with it in real situations.
It does not require special talent. Consequently, we developed
a three day course for employees of Sumitomo Electric and
affiliated companies that would allow anyone to use this
method. (In addition to this IE course [Table 5-5], we also developed courses in quality control and production control.)

5.5 ACHIEVING IMPROVEMENT THROUGH PRACTICE

The IE course was intended to teach the following lesson: In
spite of the numerous texts we have on IE, and the fact that

many people possess great knowledge of IE methods, there still remains much room for improvement in blue collar as well as white collar jobs. If you observe a job through analytical eyes, it is not difficult to find waste in the way it is being done.

I suppose that many readers have had a similar experience, that is, applying the techniques of IE to analyze a problem, without a significant measure of success. When results do not merit the time and effort we have invested, we often become discouraged with them. In fact, it is not at all exceptional to see two industrial engineers spend six months developing an idea that will economize one worker and may never even be put into practice. Since IE should be a tool for solving problems effectively and efficiently, it is no wonder that we become quite discouraged with such experiences.

One of the important lessons that we learned is that the cause of failure should not be attributed to the IE methods themselves or to our knowledge and understanding of them, but rather to insufficient practice. We must practice IE methods enough so that we become capable of spotting opportunities for improvement at a glance.

It is often difficult, however, to have sufficient time to practice IE applications and still perform one's own work. After having learned basic IE methods, we must make an effort to practice them within the limited time that is available to us. The best way to do this is to observe daily operations around us consciously and analytically.

For this observation, we must be sure to watch just which parts of a worker's body move (Figure 5-3), and locate inefficient motions by comparing them to the principles of motion economy (Table 5-4). Such a conscious and analytical attitude is called motion mind in the field of industrial engineering.

IE defines those who have motion mind in the following three levels:

(1) Find differences among different motions (find and detect problems).

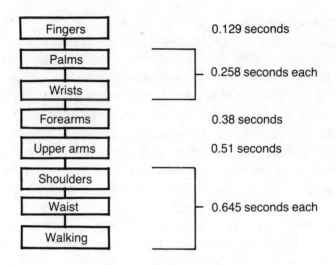

Figure 5-3 Body Motions and Average Time Required

(2) Decide which motion is preferable (explain the reason).

(3) Develop a superior motion (develop an improvement).

If you practice observing motion (not only in the plant but in the office as well) with motion mind, you will gradually become able to detect inefficient motion quite easily. Such practice does not take much time. Once an inefficient motion is detected, the desire will appear to eliminate it. This is the driving force for improvement.

You should not tackle a large problem right after learning a basic IE method. Rather, you should practice observing with motion mind on a daily basis, finding and solving the problems you detect, however small they may be. Daily operations provide a good opportunity for practicing IE methods this way.

Once you have developed the capability to achieve improvement through this practice, you can also help those around you develop motion mind. Find inefficient elements in their work, explain why these elements are inefficient, and show how to make the necessary improvements. It is impossible for foremen to spot every inefficient element in every worker's motion even if they do possess excellent motion mind. We cannot expect them alone to raise the overall productivity of an entire plant.

If, on the other hand, all of the workers possess motion mind and try to improve their own work, improvements will be much accelerated with remarkable results. No matter how small each worker's individual role may be, a large population with motion mind can achieve far larger effects on the entire company than a limited number of distinguished engineers. Figure 5-4 illustrates my idea about the difference.

It is not easy to increase labor productivity by 50%. I recommend to readers that they try to estimate how much investment is needed for 50% productivity growth. They might doubt me if I say that we achieved it with little investment and without forcing workers to work harder. The fact is that we did obtain these impressive results through IE and motion mind. We must not overlook this approach and set off on a hasty path of massive investments in robotization and automation. IE improvements must provide the basis for robots and automation.

5.6 POINTS ON THE OBSERVATION OF OPERATIONS

The following points on the observation of operations should be noted:

(1) All employees must understand the reasons for operations improvement. If one tries to measure and improve an operation with a stopwatch or video tape recorder without giving an appropriate explanation to the people who are concerned, he will obtain neither their participation nor accurate data. It is indispensable to provide an adequate understanding of the goals and purpose of operations improvement. The

improvement target should be determined through total participation.

(2) The observed worker must understand the purpose of observation. Most workers are unable to relax while their operations are being measured. They may also misunderstand the reason they are being observed. I once witnessed a case where a worker was too anxious to continue his soldering work because he had not been given any explanation beforehand. I felt sorry for him.

It is essential to provide a satisfactory explanation for observation and measurement in order to have the workers continue to work as usual. Operations observation and time measurement are conducted to find time differences between different methods, not to compare operation speeds between workers.

However hard a worker works, he will be unable to raise productivity significantly if his work method involves many inefficient elements. On the contrary, high productivity is possible if a work method is itself efficient. Although it is difficult to measure accurately the ease and efficiency of an operation, the time needed to perform it can be one reliable measure.

(3) An actual operation should be observed in detail. We do not necessarily know every detail of operations, even in our own plant. This is because we do not have actual work experience, or different workers perform the same operation differently. In the latter case, we must determine the reason for these differences. Workers know about their methods for performing different operations better than foremen in most cases.

As seen in the cases of CEDAC applications, we often find that workers' methods often deviate widely from standard procedures which may be impossible to follow in real work conditions. Or one may observe that workers take more time than had been expected to adjust old, worn-out equipment. In such

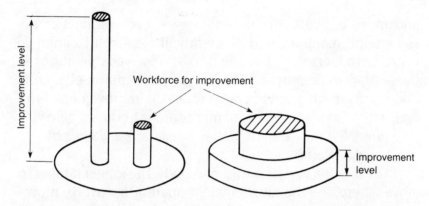

Figure 5-4   Accumulation of Small Improvements by Large Workforce

cases we must solve problems that obstruct efficient operations. For this purpose too, we must observe every detail of current operations first.

Detailed observation is easy, but seldom practiced. Analyzing elemental operations is good practice in observation. Even a little practice is enough for mastering basic operations analysis.

These detailed observations must be made for at least thirty minutes. In this process, many items requiring improvement are detected. Although these may turn out to be minor improvements, their aggregate effects are considerable. Elemental operations analysis is discussed in most textbooks on IE. Those readers interested in pursuing this subject can consult any one of them.

5.7   PRINCIPLES FOR THE IMPROVEMENT OF OPERATIONS

One often hears such statements as: "Recent order sizes are decreasing, and automation is accordingly becoming more and more difficult. Furthermore, since each product is designed and manufactured differently, it's difficult to improve overall productivity." However, if one observes operations in these plants carefully, he will find some common elemental operations leaving considerable room for improvement. Principles for discovering such elements are introduced below.

Principle 1. *Use the principles of motion economy to detect wasteful motions.*

The larger a part of the human body, the longer it takes to move. Therefore, the most efficient operations involve movements of fingers only (Figure 5-3). Such ideas are systematized in the principles of motion economy shown in Table 5-4. These principles are useful in finding wasteful elements in human motions.

One may feel, when observing a production job, that "it's tiring," "it's slow," or "it doesn't have any rhythm." In such cases, it is possible to determine what elements are wasteful by consulting these principles. This simple method will help eliminate wasteful elements in many cases.

The principles of motion economy also enable us to observe operations in a new way, that is, to compare them with ideal conditions. It is not so difficult to imagine ideal operations. Consider an assembly operation, for instance. One should be able to pick up the necessary parts quickly and with a minimum of movement. The assembly job should not involve checking part types, assembly positions, adjustments or repairs. The worker must be in a natural posture, moving his arms and legs with good balance. When the assembly has been completed, the goods should be transferred to the next process within a minimum distance. In other words, the ideal operation involves only those elements that add value to the product. All other elements should be eliminated. Comparing the ideal operation with the present method, one may easily detect which aspects of an operation should be improved.

Basic Principles	Hints for Improvement	Basics for Motion	Basics for Work Environment	Basics for Tools
Utilize both hands simultaneously.	Eliminate waiting, balancing, and holding.	Both hands start and finish at the same time. Both hands move symmetrically.	Design layout so that both hands move simultaneously.	Use devices for holding goods for a long period of time. For simple operations, or those requiring power, use devices operated by foot.
Minimize the number of movements.	Eliminate searching, choosing, carrying, thinking, placing, and re-grasping. Facilitate grasping and assembling.	Eliminate unnecessary movements. Reduce number of required movements; combine two movements or more.	Place tools and materials in the order of use. Place tools and materials so as to facilitate their use.	Use appropriate containers for parts. Use fixing devices with fewer nuts and bolts. Combine two tools into one.
Minimize the distance of each movement.	Reduce arm's motions. Reduce waist's motions. Reduce walking distances.	Minimize the parts of the body that move. Use the appropriate part of the body.	Minimize work area, without obstructing body movements. Place tools and material as near as possible.	Use gravity to transfer goods.
To facilitate movement:	Eliminate jobs that require power, unnatural posture, or concentration. Eliminate changing and adjusting material positions. Eliminate difficult movements.	Use basic, natural movements. Make movements smooth and natural. Use natural powers (gravity, inertia, etc.)	Optimize the height of the worktable.	Use tools and guide to control movements. Use power-operated tools.

Table 5-4 Principles of Motion Economy

Case 1 in the appendix shows how an operation was improved by applying the principles of motion economy.

Principle 2. Analyze the necessity of the operation.

Many operations considered necessary can in fact be simplified or even eliminated if they are approached from a different viewpoint. Detailed and analytical observation is essential for this purpose. Areas for improvement are detected through the process of analyzing each elemental operation's necessity and objective. Ideas obtained in this way often eliminate an entire operation.

Analyzing necessity is straightforward enough. One has only to ask a series of questions such as: "Why do I perform this operation?" "Why do I do it in this order?" "Why do I have to check it?" The answers to these questions determine the necessity of a given operation.

Such questioning is often proposed in plants, but most people stop at this stage and obtain only limited results. The next step is more important: to develop many alternative ways of reaching the same objective. For example, "Can I include it in the previous process?" "Is there another way I can do it without adjustment?" "Can I eliminate it completely?" and so on.

If one attacks a large operation as a whole, he will find that it includes various necessary elements and is very hard to improve. Dividing it down to the level of elemental operations or even unit movements is the key to generating an abundance of new improvement ideas. Such a process can produce astonishing ideas for improvement (see Case 2 in the Appendix to this chapter).

Principle 3. Observe the previous and subsequent processes together.

Principles 1 and 2 aim at improvement in a single process. However, many improvements may be secured by observing subsequent processes at the same time. This type of improvement has a greater effect in most cases. Clues for this type of

improvement include:
- The placing and picking up of products are done separately between the two processes
- The two processes can be integrated
- The two processes can be divided differently
- One worker can be assigned to the two processes
- An operation can be transferred to a different process
- The work can be divided differently between workers so that all the workers have the same cycle time. This often requires changing equipment layouts, as seen in Case 3.

Improvements are often made by means of these concepts. For example, a delivered product is dismantled for the inspection of inner parts, reassembled and then taken apart for other checks, etc. Extreme division of labor often causes such wasteful operations.

It should be noted that most advanced machine tools can be used to perform a variety of operations once they hold a product. Picking up and placing operations must be kept to a minimum. They are wasteful operations and tend to exacerbate unnecessary costs.

5.8   AN INVITATION TO IE IMPROVEMENT

The reader may suspect that the method introduced above is too old-fashioned for today's rapidly changing world. He might prefer more drastic measures suitable to this age of automation. A powerful medicine may be effective in the short run, but it cannot create lasting physical strength. I do not deny the necessity of such medicine in certain cases, but I am afraid that people, longing for such medicine, overlook many improvement opportunities right under their noses.

I briefly introduced a method which can give power to people for solving problems on the job. If a company obtains such improvement power, it can grow anywhere, no matter what problems it must surmount. If its competitive advantage lies only in equipment, its competitors can easily catch up with it by making the same investment. No company can rely solely on capital investment to improve productivity. If it possesses some strength which takes a long time to develop, its rivals will need an equally long period. Such strength can provide the basis of a long-lasting competitive advantage.

There is another important point. A new technique, no matter how old-fashioned it may appear, is nothing less than an engineering improvement if it allows us to increase productivity by 50% without making large capital investments or increasing work intensity. If you obtain improvement power through the method described above, you will find similar seeds for further engineering development in your own work.

5.9   THE CONTRIBUTION OF WORKER GROUP
ACTIVITIES

Once there was a time when terms such as "modern IE" or "advanced IE" were very popular. To differentiate between them, people coined a funny term, "traditional IE." Since science and engineering keep advancing, the adjectives "modern" and "advanced" really do not make much sense. Whatever the value of this term, the concept I will introduce below belongs to the realm of traditional IE.

It also concerns the QC circle activities of our Japanese workers which are now world-famous. I wonder if the reader knows that two-thirds of the improvement proposals made by worker groups are developed by traditional IE methods. This chapter introduces an engineering approach to the activities of worker groups.

The remarkable results observed in so many Japanese firms are attributed to those basic traditional IE methods rather than to group activities. The latter constitute a medium for the application of IE methods. This idea is illustrated in Table 5-5. Although production engineers may not be as interested in traditional IE methods as in robots and microcomputers, in fact they are the actual driving force behind our productivity growth.

On the other hand, it would be a mistake to overlook the impact of worker group activities on human relations. Communication and cooperation between workers and managers are improved, and opportunities for self-improvement are promoted.

Returning to productivity, we wanted to determine quantitatively how much of a contribution worker groups made relative to the contributions of our engineering staff. We used a statistical method called multiple regression analysis to explain man-hour efficiency growth by worker group activities (represented by the number of improvement suggestions per man-year). The Production Engineering Department compared this to efficiency growth, which was measured by capital investment in equipment. Data were collected from nine plants over a period of three years. Figure 5-5 shows this model.

The number of proposals is annotated with "as a representative of the aggregate measure," because it represents an aggregate measure which was developed out of twenty-seven variables concerning the plant's management and improvement power. These variables include quantitative factors such as the number of proposals, hours of group meetings, hours spent on worker education and training. They also included qualitative factors such as how group activities were activated, how we followed up on group projects and how workers were motivated. The aggregate measure developed from these variables showed the highest correlation with the number of proposals, so the latter was chosen to represent the former as an easily understandable measure.

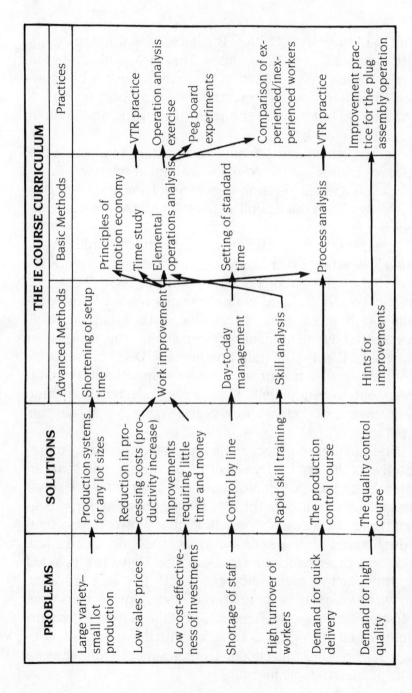

Table 5-5 Problems and the IE Course Curriculum

$$Y = 8.46 \sqrt{X_1} + 14.66 \sqrt{X_2} - 2.78$$

Y = MH efficiency growth (%/year) (or, annual average MH efficiency of the year less that of the previous year)

X_1 = Number of improvement proposals per man-year as a representative of the aggregate measure

X_2 = Capital investment on equipment ($1000/man-year)

Figure 5-5   A Regression Model for Efficiency Growth

The results of Figure 5-5 are graphed in Figure 5-6. In the figure, arrow A shows the additional amount of capital investment required to raise annual productivity growth from 20 to 25%. Arrow B shows the number of proposals needed to secure the same effect. Rather than depend only on one or the other, a combination of both, shown as arrow C, proves to be the most effective means of boosting productivity.

Another point this figure shows is that one proposal has the equivalent effect on productivity growth as a $3,000 capital investment. However, we found that most improvement suggestions cannot produce such a significant improvement effect. We analyzed the question as follows.

As Figure 5-7 shows, the true contribution of worker groups to efficiency comes from the combination of their improvements and day-to-day management.

Day-to-day management is a system that supports worker group activities. As seen in Figure 5-7, standard times are set for current work methods, and man-hour efficiency is mea-

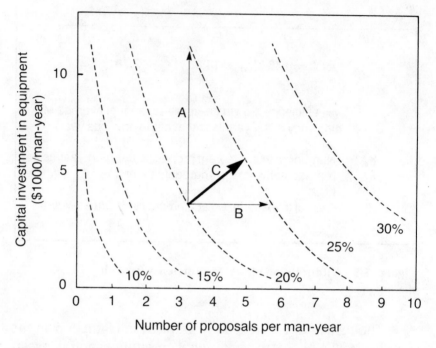

Figure 5-6 Contributions to MH Efficiency Growth

sured against them on a daily basis. The information on their man-hour efficiency is fed back to workers for their next improvement. After each improvement in work methods, standard times are revised.

Day-to-day management was developed to respond to the need for higher efficiency in production management during an age of slow economic growth. This approach requires the constant monitoring of production efficiency and quick corrective action whenever a problem is detected. Weekly or monthly monitoring suffices for evaluating overall efficiency, but not for taking adequate corrective action. Monthly monitoring makes it difficult to analyze current problems and act promptly.

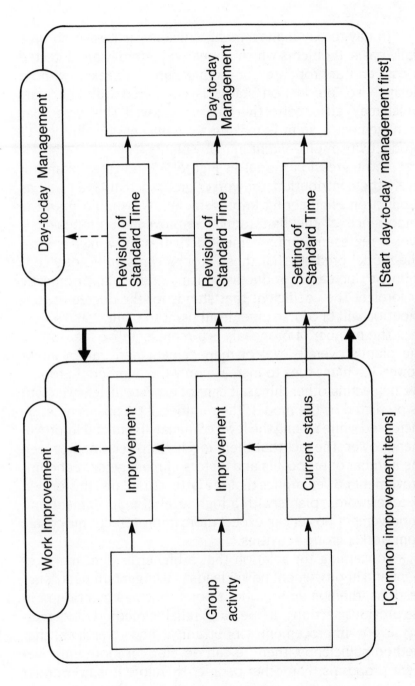

[Common improvement items]   [Start day-to-day management first]

Figure 5-7 Basic Framework for Productivity Improvement

In day-to-day management, efficiency is measured on a daily basis. Problems which appeared yesterday are detected today, and appropriate countermeasures are taken without delay. Also, production status is compared with the plan, which may call for corrective measures as well. This day-to-day management system is making a significant contribution to productivity improvement in many plants.

The regression model in Figure 5-5 indicates quantitatively the contributions of worker group activities as well as production engineering improvements. We should note the importance of the first term — improvement proposals — which represents improvement activities by worker groups. The model predicts that these groups can significantly contribute to increased productivity in any kind of plant, domestic or foreign. The coefficient that stands for the degree of contribution will of course differ from plant to plant.

The number of proposals is a representative measure of the plant's overall level of management and improvement power. If a plant tries to increase only the number of proposals, neglecting other things, it cannot expect efficiency growth as predicted by the model. The number of proposals must be increased while raising the level of management and improvement power. The fact that there is a high correlation between the number of proposals and factors of management and improvement power implies that the latter stimulates the former. In other words, plants with a high level of management and improvement power can expect more improvement proposals from worker group activities.

Concerning the relation that a higher level of management and improvement power leads to a larger number of suggestions, there is an important point that was mentioned in the previous sections: If one has a reliable method for detecting every improvement opportunity, and practices that method sufficiently, then he can develop far more improvement proposals than other people. Therefore it is no wonder that higher improvement power leads to more improvement suggestions. And, as I have said in previous sections, we do possess a reliable method, IE, which gives improvement power to worker groups.

If all the workers in a plant attain this improvement power, it will become a truly amazing organization, capable of achieving tremendous victories in the quest for productivity improvement.

APPENDIX TO CHAPTER 5
THREE CASE STUDIES

Case 1

A stamping operation in which both sides of a part are stamped.

Operation prior to improvement:
  (1) Place a pallet at point A.
  (2) Get parts from the pallet and place them at B.
  (3) Get a part at B and stamp on its upper face.
  (4) Put the part at C.
  (5) Turn the part and transfer it to B.
  (6) Get a part from B and stamp its lower face.
  (7) Put the part at C.
  (8) Transfer parts from C to the pallet.

This operation involves unnecessary steps, namely, (2), (5) and (8).

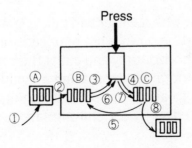

Operation after improvement:

    (1) Place a pallet at A. (Use rimless pallets to facilitate picking up).

    (2) Get a part from the pallet and stamp upper face.

    (3) Put the stamped part at B. (Finish all the parts.)

    (4) Get a part from B; turn and stamp it.

    (5) Put the part on the pallet at A.

Having eliminated unnecessary placing and picking motions, efficiency was improved by 50%.

Press

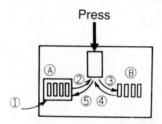

Case 2

A material cutting operation in which material for silver contacts is cut with a power cutter. The worker sandpapers an edge of material after each cutting. He was asked the following questions:

    Q: Why do you sandpaper the material?

    A: To remove scrap.

    Q: Why do you remove scrap?

    A: If there is scrap at the edge, I cannot cut the material vertically.

Material is cut with a cutter and guideboard as shown on the left panel. If cutting scrap is not removed, the material cannot be positioned horizontally and cut at the correct angle. An improvement was obtained by making a small gutter on the guide board so as to allow correct positioning of material in spite of the rough edge. By eliminating sandpapering, the average cycle time of .34 minutes was reduced by 50% to .17 minutes.

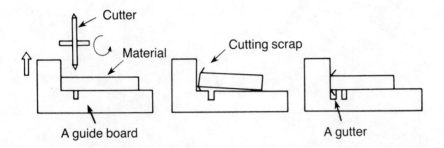

Cutter
Material
A guide board
Cutting scrap
A gutter

Case 3

A drum-rim repair operation. After electric cables are installed, their drums are dismantled and returned to the manufacturer. Before re-use, these drums are repaired if any flaw or distortion is detected on inspection.

Operation prior to improvement:
  (1) Assemble a drum.
  (2) The assembly man inspects the drum by turning it and decides if it needs repair.
  (3) Non-defective drums are sent to the paint shop.
  (4) Defective drums are transferred to the distortion repair machine.
  (5) The repairman turns the defective drum, detects distortion and repairs it.
  (6) After repair, drums are sent to the paint shop.

  In this operation, the transfer and inspection at (4) and (5) are pointless. The same inspection is done twice by two people. After improvement, the repair machine was moved to the assembly worker so that he could repair defective drums right after inspection.

Chapter 6

TWO APPROACHES TO "PRACTICE BY ALL"

6.1   OET: UTILIZING ERRORS FOR PRACTICE

Only when everyone has mastered a reliable method through constant practice can permanent positive results be attained. In the case introduced below, a system called OET (On-Error Training) was developed as a way of training workers to learn from their errors. The underlying principle of OET is that workers can best learn to improve quality and productivity by studying their mistakes and systematically practicing a method for correcting them.

The forming section of the plant that developed OET produces 1,300 types (180,000 units) of sintered alloy parts each month. Setup operations in this section occur as many as 13,000 times a month. Semi-finished products before sintering are as brittle as chalk, so many chips and cracks appear in them. Also, since products shrink in the sintering process, size abnormalities are often observed. It is necessary for the workers in this plant to have the skill to decide appropriate methods and orders of processing as well as the skill to handle products very carefully.

Because of these difficulties, many defects due to careless work were produced — even by veteran workers. The defects included incorrect sizes, angles and shapes, as well as

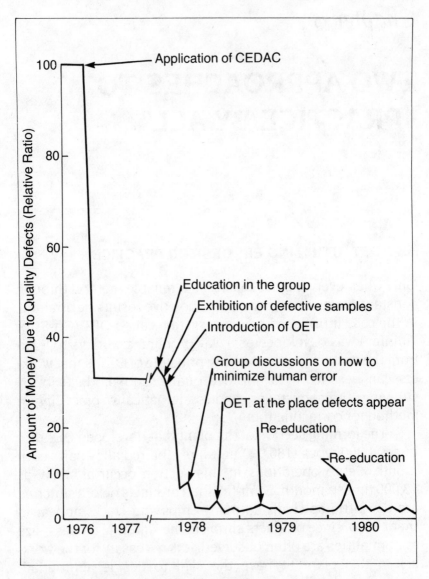

Figure 6-1   Trend of Work-In-Process Quality Defects

chips and cracks, caused by a lack of basic knowledge such as the ability to read drawings or use simple measurement tools. This resulted from inadequate on-the-job training and weaknesses in operations standards.

In mid-1976, CEDAC was introduced to this plant along with programs designed to provide basic knowledge and on-the-job training. As a result, losses due to defects were cut by two-thirds (Figure 6-1). This level continued through the latter half of1977, and was considered the minimum level attainable.

Nonetheless, the repeated appearance of defects indicated that there was still room for improvement in communications, training, standards and morale. To analyze the true causes of these defects, the New Joharry's Window described in Chapter 3 was used. Figure 6-2 was developed by four group leaders and several veteran workers. They analyzed past defect records issued during January and February of 1978, and classified each defect into one of four categories given in the window.

It turned out that there were more defects in categories II and III than in IV, which indicated that the causes of most defects were known to some employees. Some workers knew how to do their jobs correctly, but this knowledge was not adequately communicated to the others who thus continued to make mistakes.

There are several reasons why a worker may not correctly perform an operation that he knows well. He may make careless or human errors. He may not have sufficient skill to follow the correct operations. He may even consciously deviate from them.

In addition to analyzing these problems with the New Joharry's Window, workers were trained in the basic knowledge they needed to perform their jobs correctly. Starting in May 1978, defects which cropped up were exhibited for a month to increase the workers' awareness of them. This helped reduce

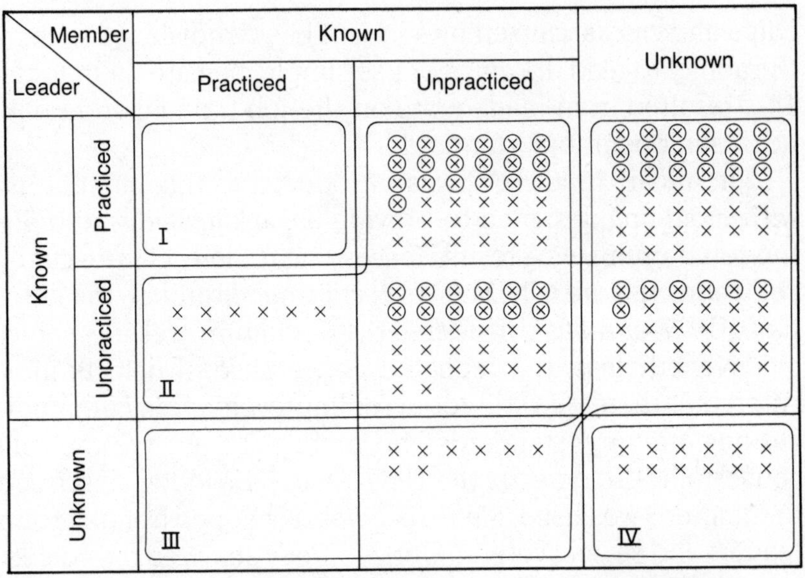

Figure 6-2   Analysis of Failure by OET (January-February 1978)

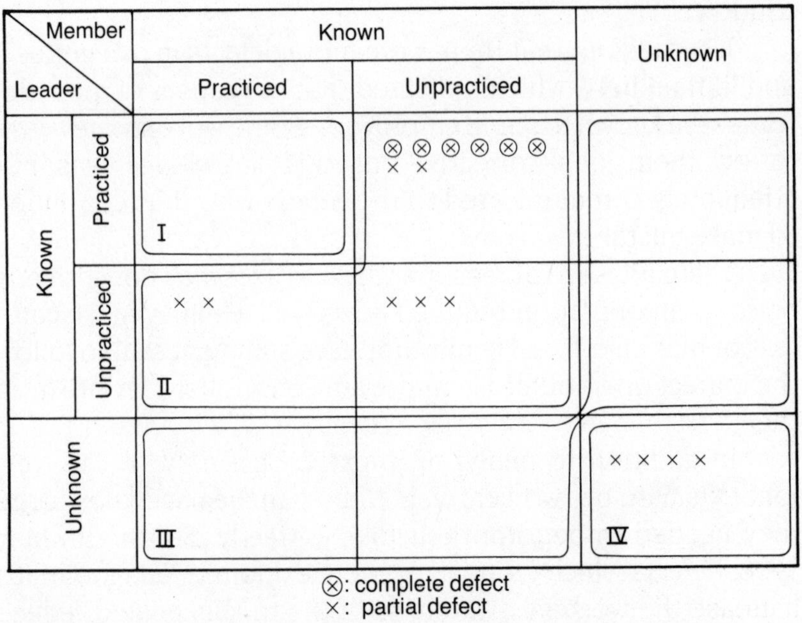

⊗: complete defect
×: partial defect

Figure 6-3   Analysis of Failure by OET (January-February 1979)

defects considerably, but they were still not completely eliminated.

At this time the workers were divided into two groups and
had many heated discussions on whether carelessness, which
led to errors in reading drawings and choosing correct tools,
could be completely eliminated. One group insisted that it
was impossible. The other believed that careless errors could
be removed if their causes were eliminated. The OET activities
were instituted to focus this heightened awareness on defect
reduction. Our goal was to have all the workers think and teach
each other as soon as any defect was detected. We intended to
utilize defects as good opportunities to teach and practice correct operations.

Five rules were established for on-error training:

(1) The *quickly* rule
(2) The *actually* rule
(3) The *himself* rule
(4) The *don't speak* rule
(5) The *support* rule

The quickly rule requires that the person who caused the
defect call all the group members within thirty minutes to discuss countermeasures. This meeting would not last for more
than thirty minutes.

The actually rule requires the person who caused the defect to play back the operation, exactly as he had done it, to the
group. Causes and countermeasures are also discussed in the
same place. This makes it easier for the others to understand
how and why the defect occurred.

The himself rule requires the person who caused the
defect to explain it to the others himself.

The don't speak rule prohibits foremen and group leaders
from speaking first. It aims at giving other people a chance to
speak, because if the foremen or leaders present their ideas
first, other members may not think by themselves and may feel
inhibited.

Foremen and leaders are only allowed to speak at the final stage of the meeting. They are expected to support group activities behind the scene. This is called the support rule.

As a result of these rules, discussions and improvement by the worker groups came about more frequently than we had originally expected. Figure 6-3 shows the result of OET after it had been running for four months. Compared with the data of Figure 6-2, it is easily seen that defects had been drastically reduced.

In ordinary worker training programs, workers tend to be passive. In OET, on the other hand, they are expected to actively teach each other. This is the reason we use the word "practice," which has an active connotation, rather than "training," which suggests passivity.

OET is a method for building quality control activities out of daily work, and it suggests a new direction for QC. Its four essential elements are shown in Figure 6-4, and it is compared to ordinary group activities in Table 6-1.

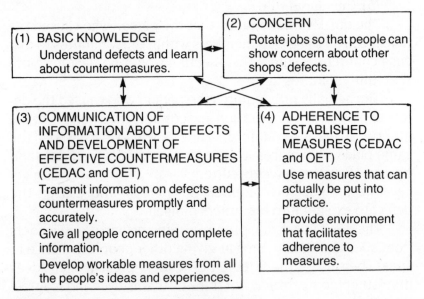

Figure 6-4   Four Essential Factors for OET

	PREVIOUS GROUP ACTIVITIES	**OET**
When	Once a month	Within 30 minutes of appearance of defect
Where	In a meeting room	At the shop where a defect appears
Called by	Foreman	The person who caused the defect
Presided by	Foreman	Group leader or the person concerned
Speakers	Mostly foreman and group leader	Everyone except foreman and group leader
Man-hours spent	40 MH/month	From 19.0-40.5 MH/month
Proposals	Inactive	Active
Graphs watched	Infrequently	Every day
Losses calculated by	Foreman or group leader	By the person concerned
Job rotations	Not welcome	Welcome
Concerns for quality	Low	High
Information sought	Inactively	Actively
Knowledge sought	Inactively	Actively

Table 6-1   Comparison of OET and Previous Group Activities

A worker once said to me: "We were afraid we were spending too much time on OET. At the outset, we spent 190 man-hours per month, which equalled 3% of the section's total man-hours. But as we took effective measures one after the other, man-hours for OET decreased; the present level is 40.5 man-hours, or .6% of the total."

Thus we learned the importance of investing in education and practice from the OET experience.

6.2 PRACTICING QC BY THE CASE METHOD

Many, many QC methods have been developed, and they are taught in many seminars and textbooks in Japan. Unfortunately, these methods are not often used effectively in real manufacturing situations. The importance of seminars and textbooks for teaching QC cannot be over-emphasized, but we also need efficient methods for practicing it. The best way to practice QC methods is to apply them to actual problems. However, most people, without good coaching, do not have the wherewithal to go through this long trial-and-error process.

To achieve a breakthrough, we developed a case method for QC. Participants in this case method are expected to apply their QC knowledge and methods to a fictional problem, and to learn how to correct their weaknesses by studying their failures and listening to the instructor's advice.

This case method is adopted in a three-day QC program for staff and managers within the company. About 300 people participated in this program. They were divided into sixteen classes, each with fewer than twenty members. The program questionnaire we developed for participants showed that the case method was ranked among the most popular courses. We often heard comments such as: "It was very helpful." "My confidence has been restored." "Now I understand why our former

QC activities were not fruitful."

Encouraged by this result, the third session of the managers' QC Convention of the Japanese Union of Scientists and Engineers (where I serve as chairman) is now studying techniques for developing good practice cases.

I would like to comment here on the case method. As is widely known, the case method originated at Harvard Business School as a unique approach to business education. Wallace B. Donham, who was dean of the business school for twenty-four years, laid the foundations of the case method. All the courses at the school are taught according to this method, which has earned renown as a landmark innovation in education. Since I have never witnessed the Harvard method in action, I am not certain whether our own method differs from it.

It has often been noted that learning only from lectures does little to prepare us for the practical application of that knowledge in real situations. Once a new graduate joined a company and was taken aback when his boss said to him: "What can you do for us?" Since we spend a lot of time obtaining knowledge at school as well as in the company, we expect good results that justify our efforts.

One might be tempted to reply that good textbooks contain questions and exercises for learning QC. I do not deny the necessity of exercises, but they differ from the case method on the following points: The exercise question provides all the information necessary to solve it, and it has only one right solution. What is more, most of the examinations given in schools have only one correct solution (at least from the teacher's point of view).

On the other hand, our case method does not give all the information, and there may be more than one solution. In fact, the more knowledge and information one has, the more solutions he may discover.

In addition, solutions to case method problems can be assigned priorities according to their effectiveness. The reasons behind these priorities must be very clear if they are to persuade case participants. Finding as many solutions as possible and assigning them reasonable priorities are necessary conditions for securing good results, not only in QC but in all other fields.

Few real problems in business provide all the necessary information. Thus we are always constrained to making decisions in a context of uncertainty. We have to estimate unknown factors to apply basic decision-making models.

In the three-day program mentioned above, teams of four to five people are requested to write out their judgments and countermeasures for a case during the morning of the first day. From then on to the afternoon of the last day, the group listens to lectures. Then the same case is tried again by the same people. They are expected to see how different their judgments and proposals are following the lectures. Since the participants are all able managers and staff, their proposals on the first day are not necessarily poor, but if they are able to note a difference between their first and second tries, however slight, they will recognize the effectiveness of the education.

One particular suggestion from the instructor was well received by all the participants: "In the past you have applied QC methods at the level of the first trial. If you observed an improvement after the lectures, then you had better practice QC at that level from now on. This difference can be capitalized upon as your competitive advantage over rival companies."

The difference between the first and second trial is due to:
- Lack of basic knowledge, or insufficient practice for applying the knowledge that a participant did possess
- Jumping to vague conclusions or proposals without rigorously analyzing the causes
- Over-generalization
- Neglect of an action that should and can be taken immediately, possibly because of over-generalization

- Lack of understanding of the importance of mathematical techniques in QC
- Blind belief in amateurish approaches to QC

Since there were abundant opportunities to learn QC in Japan, mere lectures were not enough to attract the interest of the participants. They already knew most of the methods and theories. Therefore, the case method was employed to help them realize the critical importance of knowing reliable methods and mastering them through practice.

The more competent one is, the fewer opportunities he has to have his weaknesses in QC pointed out to him in his daily work. Highly able staff and managers can increase their QC skill levels best by using the case method.

I observed an interesting fact through the case method. That is, competent people have a very clear perception of their weaknesses. On the other hand, those with insufficient knowledge and ability do not readily learn from their failures. There is an obvious causal relationship between one's ability and his sensitivity to feedback. Those with an effective feedback "circuit" can learn from failures, improve their weaknesses, and correct their mistakes, thus becoming increasingly able. I expect some participants learned something from reflecting on their past failures and weaknesses in QC. Such a profound lesson can be learned only from within.

I also employ a case method for the final examination of the reliability engineering course I teach at the Department of Systems Engineering at Kobe University. I have been lecturing at this school with its cheerful, liberal character and beautiful mountainside campus since 1975. And it has been a great pleasure for me to work with such dedicated students.

The final examination begins like this:

You are a reliability engineer hired by F.R. Bisman, an automobile engine manufacturer based in West Germany. You belong to the Production Engineering Department of the third plant. The foreman of the inspection process and the chief of the final engine assembly shop reported a problem as described in the attached sheet. They asked the plant manager what measures should be taken. The manager wants advice from you as a reliability engineer. Describe your proposals briefly. This is your first job at this company. I hope you do a good job.

The fact that a German company is used is not important. I was just afraid that the students would be influenced by their biases if it were a Japanese firm.

As a result of this preparation, I have full confidence that my students will be able to do a good job when their future bosses ask them: "You took a course in reliability engineering; what can you do to improve this product's reliability?"

Chapter 7

SITUATIONAL ANALYSIS: FIND YOUR PROBLEMS YOURSELF

In Chapter 1 I described a case in which a situation favorable to improvements was developed by demonstrating the effectiveness of IE methods. The existence of reliable methods as well as sufficient practice of them is important in the development of such a favorable situation.

To create a favorable environment, correct situational analysis is indispensable.

7.1 CARTOONS FOR EQUIPMENT MAINTENANCE

Production equipment cannot be used to its full effectiveness without the close cooperation of machine operators and maintenance workers. In heavy industries, this equipment actually produces the products, so equipment maintenance is the most important factor in production engineering.

When I was manager of the equipment development and maintenance section of an alloy products plant, I tried to develop a Total Preventive Maintenance (TPM) system in which machine operators and maintenance workers work together. I first interviewed a maintenance worker. He said: "We are machine repairmen, but are the operators machine destroyers?" Human relations between operators and maintenance workers were not very friendly. In this situation, it was not a good strategy to strengthen only one party. I wanted to improve both groups' skills and knowledge at the same time.

The first thing I did was ask the maintenance workers to draw cartoons to express what they wanted the operators to do. Fortunately, there was a very good artist among them who drew twenty poster-size cartoons. I still have several of them now, nine years later. For example, one cartoon presents the machine as a child, with the operator as its mother. The mother brought the child to the doctor (the maintenance worker), complaining that the child had a headache. But the child's sickness was actually in its abdomen, and the doctor, having been misled by the mother, had to go to great lengths to find the true sickness. Other cartoons illustrated machines crying because of lack of oiling, and a drive shaft worn out by dust.

The cartoons were exhibited in the plant. After that, I summarized everyone's ideas in the form shown in Figure 7-1. (Although this form resembles Professor Kawakita's KJ method, it did not follow the same formal steps.)

7.2   REPLACING FORMAL MEETINGS

Figure 7-1 was drawn as follows: After exhibiting the cartoons, I asked the operators and maintenance workers (who at that time belonged to a different section), to write down their own ideas for improved equipment maintenance. They were expected to write down one suggestion per card, and the number of cards was unlimited.

A few days later, many cards were collected. I read them

over again and again. By rereading, I was able to grasp the situation which was explained in diverse ways on the cards.

I sorted the cards into several groups and gave each group a short title. The cards were posted on a large chart where everyone could read them. I then asked the workers to let me know if I had misunderstood what they meant on the cards. I proceeded to revise the titles until they were accepted by everyone.

Some examples of the cards are given in Figure 7-1, but all the cards were posted on the original diagram.

7.3 CLARIFYING THE PROBLEM SITUATION

There were three basic groups of cards. The upper left group included many cards indicating that what was needed for better *equipment maintenance* was not skill but rather knowledge and information. The maintenance workers wanted better information on machine breakdowns, while the machine operators demanded better explanations of the repairs. The upper right group (on the chart) concerned *equipment design*; since some of the machines were poorly designed, they often broke down and needed frequent repairs. The groups at the bottom involved items on *equipment improvements*. As a machine wears out, it needs not only repairs to restore it to its original condition, but also improvements so that it will be subject to fewer repairs in the future.

After having thus analyzed the situation, I called all the concerned staff and line workers together for a meeting to discuss concrete measures for better equipment maintenance with the full cooperation of the machine operators and maintenance workers. I realized at this time that we had usually held similar meetings without the appropriate situational analysis.

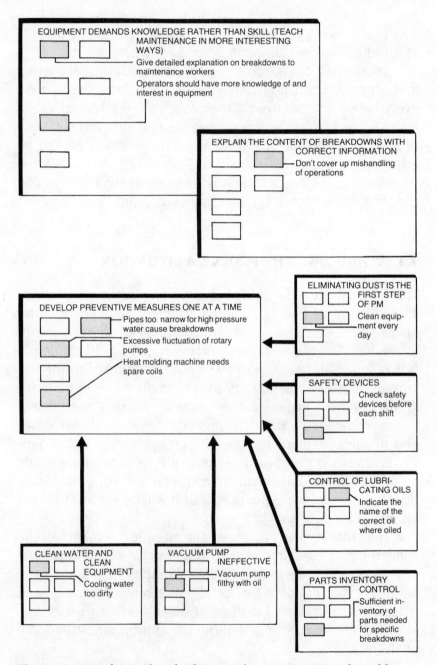

Figure 7-1 Author's Sketch of Some Ideas on TPM Developed by

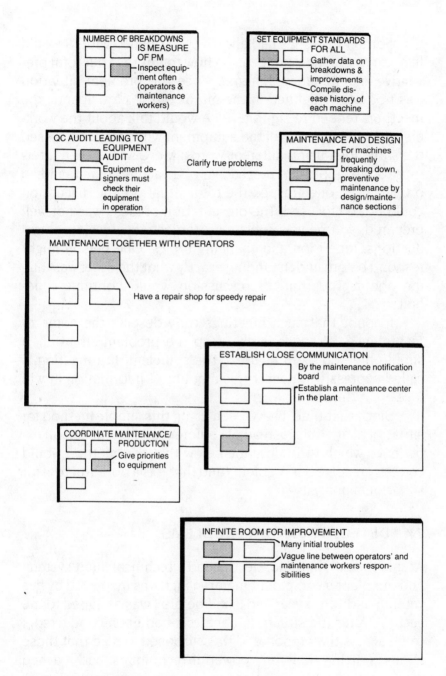

NUMBER OF BREAKDOWNS IS MEASURE OF PM
- Inspect equipment often (operators & maintenance workers)

SET EQUIPMENT STANDARDS FOR ALL
- Gather data on breakdowns & improvements
- Compile disease history of each machine

QC AUDIT LEADING TO EQUIPMENT AUDIT
- Equipment designers must check their equipment in operation

Clarify true problems

MAINTENANCE AND DESIGN
- For machines frequently breaking down, preventive maintenance by design/maintenance sections

MAINTENANCE TOGETHER WITH OPERATORS

Have a repair shop for speedy repair

ESTABLISH CLOSE COMMUNICATION
- By the maintenance notification board
- Establish a maintenance center in the plant

COORDINATE MAINTENANCE/ PRODUCTION
- Give priorities to equipment

INFINITE ROOM FOR IMPROVEMENT
- Many initial troubles
- Vague line between operators' and maintenance workers' responsibilities

Workers Using Cards

Former meetings had always been opened with: "I would like you to tell me your ideas on how to improve our total preventive maintenance system." Since the problem situation was not clearly defined in the minds of the participants, the meetings tended to zig-zag: Mr. A would talk about the workers' lack of knowledge of the equipment while Mr. B expressed the same idea using different words. Mr. C would then interrupt to talk about the breakdown of a vacuum pump, and so on. Since no one grasped the total situation, the discussion could not be focused. The presentation of ideas was not well prepared, so one was constantly subjected to useless introductions, repetition and changing topics. One person might respond before understanding exactly what the other was talking about. The fruitless discussion would continue indefinitely....

I doubt that such meetings truly deserve the name of "conference." To adequately grasp the problem situation, a simple method as in Figure 7-1 is sufficient. If a meeting is called expressly to collect this amount of information, it will take great time and effort.

Since that time, I have been using this simple method for situational analysis instead of conferences. I learned in an experience which I will describe below that this method would correctly resolve our problems and that it is a powerful tool for situational analysis.

7.4 DETECT YOUR OWN PROBLEMS

At this time, Sumitomo Electric had a technical audit system, and our plant's equipment maintenance was inspected by five veteran auditors a year and a half before I was assigned to the section. After the situational analysis had been conducted, I came across their report and was surprised to read that those auditors, using their very powerful techniques, had reached exactly the same conclusion I had by my simple method.

I learned from this experience that the method sufficed to detect problems and that we therefore needed no external auditors. When I was the manager of an IE department that included technical audits among its many tasks, several directors asked us to inspect them. Instead of accepting their invitation, I always encouraged them to conduct a situational analysis by themselves. It is almost impossible for external auditors to analyze a situation better than those who actually face it. This is based on the assumption that internal people do their best to understand their own situation.

I believe that situational analysis by people who are actually concerned is the best way to gather and integrate information correctly. And it is a powerful advantage to have a reliable method for conducting such situational analysis swiftly and correctly.

In the case of the alloy products plant, a meeting was called only when the situational analysis had been completed. The machine operators and maintenance workers were asked to develop improvement ideas based on the results of the analysis. From this analysis, it had become clear that the operators required more knowledge of the equipment. Some kind of educational program had to be developed.

7.5   CORRECT SITUATIONAL ANALYSIS AND CORRECT ACTIONS

We decided to take the following measures:

The foremen for the two maintenance groups, one for electric facilities, the other for machines, investigated breakdowns during the previous year that had been caused by insufficient worker knowledge. These covered 23% of the total machine breakdowns. They analyzed these breakdowns and wrote a short textbook for operators with basic but indispensable knowledge on equipment.

They told the operators:

"Twenty-three percent of last year's breakdowns were caused because you don't know your machines very well. We have collected very important knowledge in this notebook that we want you all to know. If you master this textbook, however hard it may be, you will be able to reduce breakdowns by 23%. Therefore, please do your best to read it."

The era of skilled veterans is over, and operators are now required to have appropriate knowledge to use sophisticated equipment. The foremen offered no comforting phrases such as: "Learning about equipment is interesting," or: "It's easy." But they did provide a scenario for success: although knowledge on equipment is hard to obtain, it can reduce breakdowns by 23%. This scenario was realized the following year, and breakdowns caused by operators' insufficient knowledge dropped from 23 to 4%.

Next, we decided to tackle breakdowns of poorly designed machines. The previous year's data showed that 17% of total breakdowns could be directly attributed to poor design. This figure might be underestimated because the foremen may have wanted to spare the designers some embarrassment. We spent seven months redesigning and improving those machines.

To facilitate this process, a system called the "equipment patrol" was devised. It required the designers to patrol the plant and inspect how the machines they had designed were working. They were expected to spend at least one day per month following up on the machines' performance, ease of maintenance, and the level and variability of product quality.

This system was a variation on the QC Patrol which I had established in the latter half of the three years when I was still manager of the Quality Assurance (QA) section. A QC Patrol team consisted of a QA manager who acted as leader, and four to five members from other sections. The team patrolled one plant each month, inspecting the QC system of the plant from the customer's viewpoint.

Since the members also had many other responsibilities, they were allowed to take business trips and leave for meetings during the patrol week, if necessary. The patrol team was requested to present the result to the manager of the division as well as managers of the plant and other concerned sections. The inspected plant had to report to management, within one month's time, on its improvement plan for any problems that had been detected.

Redesigning by engineers, in addition to the education of operators, reduced the total number of breakdowns by 35%, which was nearly what we had expected. We learned from this experience that correct situational analysis leads to correct action.

Another lesson that I learned was that the project manager must present a scenario for success based on clear reasons and factual data. It is the key to true leadership.

Chapter 8

AN INVITATION TO SELF-STUDY— FOR THE ACTIVE MIND

8.1 ON THE HAWTHORNE STUDY

In the 1950s, when Drs. Deming and Juran first brought QC to Japan, we were shocked by differences between Japan and the United States. Since then, we have been working quite hard to catch up, and now, thanks to our efforts, and blessed with favorable conditions, our quality levels have greatly improved.

Strangely enough, our efforts were stimulated by a misunderstanding. We thought that the concepts being taught to us by Drs. Deming and Juran were actually practiced by American firms. Without realizing the differences between research and practice, and between top-level companies and average companies, we made every effort to catch up with what was, in fact, an illusion. Theory Y, for example, is not so well known or applied in the U.S. as in Japan.

Our efforts to catch up brought much success, but we also realized that hard work alone was not enough to lead us to the top. Recognizing this, we developed the study group approach as a means for establishing our own managerial engineering methods and techniques. Figure 8-1 gives an overview of the study groups, only some of which are described in this book. However, I hope that this book has communicated the basic

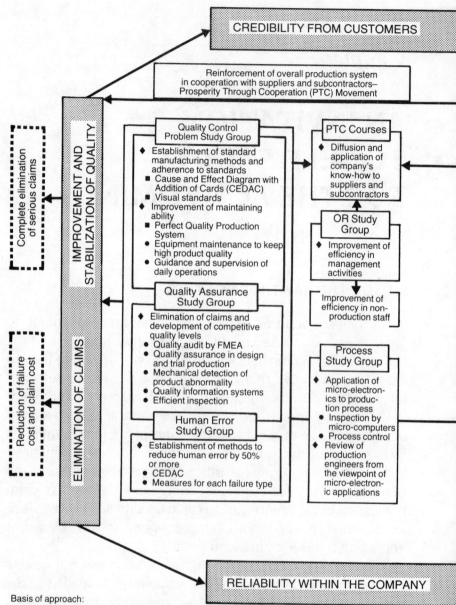

Figure 8-1 contents:

CREDIBILITY FROM CUSTOMERS

Reinforcement of overall production system in cooperation with suppliers and subcontractors— Prosperity Through Cooperation (PTC) Movement

IMPROVEMENT AND STABILIZATION OF QUALITY

ELIMINATION OF CLAIMS

Complete elimination of serious claims

Reduction of failure cost and claim cost

Quality Control Problem Study Group
♦ Establishment of standard manufacturing methods and adherence to standards
  ■ Cause and Effect Diagram with Addition of Cards (CEDAC)
  ■ Visual standards
♦ Improvement of maintaining ability
  ■ Perfect Quality Production System
  ● Equipment maintenance to keep high product quality
  ● Guidance and supervision of daily operations

Quality Assurance Study Group
♦ Elimination of claims and development of competitive quality levels
  ● Quality audit by FMEA
  ● Quality assurance in design and trial production
  ● Mechanical detection of product abnormality
  ● Quality information systems
  ● Efficient inspection

Human Error Study Group
♦ Establishment of methods to reduce human error by 50% or more
  ● CEDAC
  ● Measures for each failure type

PTC Courses
♦ Diffusion and application of company's know-how to suppliers and subcontractors

OR Study Group
♦ Improvement of efficiency in management activities

Improvement of efficiency in non-production staff

Process Study Group
♦ Application of micro-electronics to production process
  ● Inspection by micro-computers
  ● Process control
  ● Review of production engineers from the viewpoint of micro-electronic applications

RELIABILITY WITHIN THE COMPANY

Basis of approach:
(1) Development of our own know-how through the integration of knowledge and experience obtained in the above activities.
(2) Establishment of engineering (IE) which can be effectively used by any person, at any place, and at any time.

Figure 8-1   Production System Improvement Through IE Activities

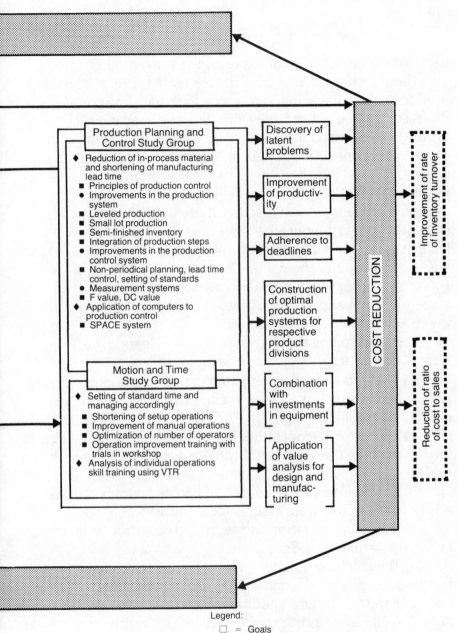

Legend:

☐ = Goals

▪▪▪ = Evaluating measures

[ ] = Subjects to be selected in the near future

♦ = Goals assigned to each study group

▪ = Systems and methods developed (or modified)
in our company, including those under development

ideas and approaches common to all the study groups.

The weakness of blind, hard work is that it may lead to overlooking the importance of adopting a specific approach. Professor J. Lee of Ohio State University criticized the Hawthorne Study as a fraud a few years ago. Dr. Marvin E. Mundel, a former president of the American Institute of Industrial Engineers, pointed out the failures of the Hawthorne study in a lecture at Osaka, Japan. One of the listeners asked some angry questions: "When did you discover these errors? Do other researchers support your theories? Did you know that all Japanese engineers believe that the Hawthorne study is the basis for managerial engineering?" For those hard workers, the Hawthorne study was the symbol of American managerial engineering. What anger they expressed when they learned that they had been betrayed by a fraud!

The Hawthorne study was discussed in Chapter 3.8. Professor Lee's criticism is summarized below:

(1) The women who participated in the experiments were not chosen at random. Among them, two were close friends chosen intentionally.

(2) The assembly operation in the test room included far fewer parts than the real assembly line, so the work was much easier.

(3) The women who were tested did not perform various additional tasks that were assigned to other assembly workers.

(4) The setup operation and supplying of parts were much facilitated in the test room.

(5) The efficiency rate plan was applied to a group of one hundred people on the main line, while it applied to five people in the test room. In addition to better supervision, this favorable rate plan encouraged the women to work harder.

(6) On the main line, workers had to go home when a stock of parts was used up. In the test room, however, stocks were well maintained.

Dr. Lee suggested that it was no wonder that efficiency was much improved under these artificial conditions.

I would like to mention two points here. One is that what we learned from the Hawthorne study was not so much the results of the experiments, but rather, the research attitude that sought to analyze an unexpected phenomenon and attempted to discover the unknown factors that caused it. This attitude was the driving force behind an enormous amount of subsequent research. Even if the Hawthorne study must be criticized from a methodological point of view, the approach we learned from it is not weakened as long as we retain confidence in our own self-study. The only point to be corrected is our understanding of the results of the Hawthorne study.

Another interesting point is that the favorable conditions that Dr. Lee criticized are just those that have been realized by Japanese productivity improvement plans. As a result, our productivity was improved exactly as Dr. Lee pointed out that the Hawthorne group's productivity should rise! Professor Lee's criticism was proven true in Japanese plants.

8.2 IMPROVING THE COMPANY'S CONSTITUTION

Just like a human being, a company has its own constitution. If a person has constitutional tendencies to catching cold, he will try to improve his physical condition through daily exercises, taking vitamins, and so forth. Of course, before he can improve himself, he has to know quite a lot about his physical constitution. In a company, in order to enhance quality and productivity, we have to observe ourselves carefully and take effective actions constantly in our daily work. This may not be easy, because a constant effort requires a strong will. It may take much time. However, I believe this is a promising way to success. Before concluding this book, I would like briefly to introduce such an effort which has been made in Meidensha

Electric Manufacturing Co. Ltd.

Through the "Q-up" (quality up) study group activities in Meidensha, we found that we could use the New Joharry's Window (see Chapter 3.9) as a powerful tool for solving quality problems. It is now called "Meiden's Window," and is used company-wide. The philosophy behind it is the same as that of the OET (On-Error Training) system (see Chapter 6.1), in which we learn from errors.

Every time we have a defect, whether it is detected within the company or through a customer's complaint, the information is fed back to the responsible section. The section analyzes the cause of the defect, discusses countermeasures, and determines what levels of the company's organization will be involved in preventing the defect from recurring.

Depending on the scope of this projected strategy, we select appropriate parties for Sections A and B in the Meiden's Window (Figure 8-2). There are many possible combinations

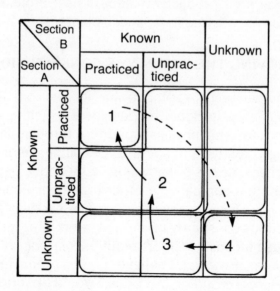

Figure 8-2 Meiden's Window

for Sections A and B. For example, when the countermeasures can be taken within one section of the company, the combination would be *section manager vs. members, skilled workers vs. new workers*, etc. When more than one section is involved, we might choose a combination such as *manufacturing department vs. design department*, or *Meidensha vs. subcontractors*, etc. The important rule is to select the best combination for facilitating mutual communication between the two parties and taking the most effective corrective actions for the defect.

The next step of the responsible section is to record the defect on the appropriate grid of the Meiden's Window. At the same time, more detailed information about the defect as well as the countermeasures are written in the form. When the defect falls into Categories 2 and 3, we use the form shown in Figure 8-3. When it falls into Category 4, the form shown in Figure 8-4 is used.

At the end of a specified period (usually a month), the results are calculated and recorded on the table shown in Figure 8-5.

In June 1982, all the serious company-wide defects and claims for the past year were classified on Meiden's Window. The data showed that the ratio among Categories 2, 3 and 4 was about 50%, 25% and 25%, respectively. Since then, we have been taking the company-wide monthly record, and the ratio has remained almost the same as in the data above.

Grasping the data led us to an epoch-making change in our basic strategies for quality problems. The problems in Categories 2 and 3 require quite different actions from those we would take for problems in Category 4. With a clear understanding of our problem areas, we became capable of implementing the right action for a given problem.

Defects in Categories 2 and 3 can be compared to a common cold. When a person catches a cold, he often takes some medicine. He may recover soon, but he is likely to catch

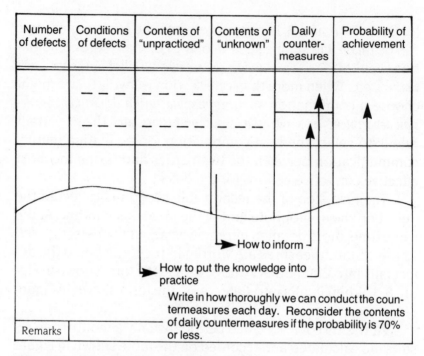

Figure 8-3   Form for Categories 2 and 3

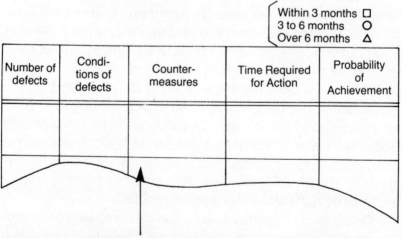

Consider the utilization of the company-wide technical data evaluation system.

Figure 8-4   Form for Category 4

Cate-gory	Number of cases			Ratio (%)	
	Inter-nal	Exter-nal	Total		
B					
C					
D					
Total				100	

Figure 8-5 Summary Table

another cold again unless he improves his physical condition. On the other hand, the defect in Category 4 is like appendicitis, or a disease curable with a specific medicine. The disease itself may be more serious than a cold, but it can be cured completely once we find and administer the correct remedy against it.

Through the use of the Meiden's Window, we reduced the number of defects by one-third from June 1982 to May 1983. The defect rate has continued to drop.

The key to successful managerial engineering is in developing a managerial system in which we can devote our constant effort to improvement. I believe that putting this effort towards a better tomorrow for the company does not mean only hardship; it can well be a source of pleasure.

POSTSCRIPT

In the present age of slow economic growth, the role of managerial engineering is bound to continue growing. By practicing managerial engineering techniques on important manufacturing problems such as setup time, quality defects and work-in-process, we learned the following: For managerial engineering to prove effective in resolving the diverse problems encountered in manufacturing operations, it must always look beyond traditional theories through the practical application of new techniques.

I have mentioned several actual cases in this book and stated that such development becomes possible when all the people who are concerned with a problem participate in its solution. Only then can their various experiences, knowledge and creativity be integrated into new methods.

These cases shed light on the methodology we developed, which is summarized as follows:
- Set an explicit goal and target for the problem
- Extract essential factors necessary for achieving the goal through practice
- Develop a new theory and method by the integration of

173

these factors with existing knowledge
- Establish a strategy to apply them
- Apply them, analyze the results and make the necessary adjustments

This book is a collection of cases in which I applied the above methodology to existing problems. In other words, managerial engineering is developed through an interdisciplinary systems approach to managerial problems.

I have stated that the driving force behind the development of managerial engineering is self-study. The backbone of self-study, in turn, is one's firm belief in the knowledge this pursuit may bring him. "Give me a fulcrum and a lever long enough and I could move the earth," Archimedes once said. He was not referring to the principle of leverage, but rather, to the power of the knowledge he had discovered through his experiments.

In conclusion, I would like to affirm that managerial engineering should seek to improve productivity while unceasingly maintaining the highest ideal of respect for humanity. In this age of low economic growth, we must take more care than ever to observe this highest of goals.

INDEX

175

About the Author

Ryuji Fukuda's book — a treasure trove of insightful ideas on industrial management — offers a new perspective on the problems that managers encounter as they try to boost quality and productivity in their facilities.

All the methods and techniques explained in these pages have stood the test of time. They have been implemented over the years at Sumitomo Electric Industries Ltd., one of Japan's leading industrial groups, and they have led to outstanding gains in productivity and quality improvement.

Ryuji Fukuda was awarded the prestigious Deming literature prize in 1978 for his contributions to the science of productivity and quality improvement.

RYUJI FUKUDA

Fukuda's career began in 1954 at the R&D division of Sumitomo Electric Industries Ltd. He joined the board of directors at Meidensha Electric Manufacturing Co. Ltd. in 1981 and was appointed general manager of the company's production facilities.

Today he is an independent consultant and advisor to Meidensha Electric and the Japan Management Association as well as to Omark Industries in Portland, Oregon and other multi-national corporations in Japan, the U.S. and Western Europe.

Born in 1928, Fukuda graduated from Kyoto University in 1954. He lectures at Kobe University on reliability engineering.

Fukuda is married and has one daughter.

Other Books on Quality Improvement

Productivity Press publishes and distributes materials on productivity, quality improvement, and employee involvement for business and industry, academia, and the general market. Many products are direct source materials from Japan that have been translated into English for the first time and are available exclusively from Productivity. Supplemental services include conferences, seminars, in-house training programs, and industrial study missions. Send for free book catalog.

Workplace Management
by Taiichi Ohno

An in-depth view of how one of this century's leading industrial thinkers approaches problem solving and continuous improvement. Gleaned from Ohno's forty years of experimentation and innovation at Toyota Motor Co., where he created JIT, this book explains the concepts that Ohno considers to be most important to successful management. A must for managing your improvement program.
ISBN 0-915299-19-4 / 166 pages / $34.95

Non-Stock Production
The Shingo System for Continuous Improvement
by Shigeo Shingo

Shingo, who developed JIT at Toyota with Taiichi Ohno, teaches how to implement non-stock production in your JIT manufacturing operations. The culmination of his extensive writings on efficient production management and continuous improvement, his latest book is an essential companion volume to his other books on key elements of JIT, and gives the most comprehensive understanding available anywhere on quality in the production function.
ISBN 0-915299-30-5 / 480 pages / $75.00

Sayings of Shigeo Shingo
Key Strategies for Plant Improvement
by Shigeo Shingo, translated by Andrew P. Dillon

Shingo's fundamental "Scientific Thinking Mechanism" (STM) was developed over 35 years of consulting for a wide variety of manufacturing operations around the world. A perfect fusion of theory and practice, with numerous anecdotes and case studies, this book will teach you the most essential problem-solving tool for your own operations. Let "Dr. Improvement" show you the way.
ISBN 0-915299-15-1 / 208 pages / $36.95

Productivity Press, Dept. BK, P.O. Box 3007, Cambridge, MA 02140 1-800-274-9911

Zero Quality Control
Source Inspection and the Poka-yoke System
by Shigeo Shingo, translated by Andrew P. Dillon

A remarkable combination of source inspection (to detect errors before they become defects) and mistake-proofing devices (to weed out defects before they can be passed down the production line) eliminates the need for statistical quality control. Shingo shows how this proven system for reducing defects to zero turns out the highest quality products in the shortest period of time. With over 100 specific examples illustrated. (Audio-visual training program also available.)
ISBN 0-915299-07-0 / 305 pages / $65.00

TQC Wisdom of Japan
Managing for Total Quality Control
by Hajime Karatsu, translated by David J. Lu

As productivity goes up, the cost of quality comes down. And as quality improves, the cost to produce comes down. Karatsu, winner of a Deming Prize who has been involved with the quality movement in Japan since its inception, discusses the purpose and techniques of Total Quality Control (TQC), how it differs from QC, and why it is so effective. There is no better introduction to TQC than this book; essential reading for all American managers.
ISBN 0-915299-29-1 / 176 pages / $34.95

Canon Production System
Creative Involvement of the Total Workforce
compiled by the Japan Management Association

A fantastic success story! Canon set a goal to increase productivity by three percent per month — and achieved it! The first book-length case study to show how to combine the most effective Japanese management principles and quality improvement techniques into one overall strategy that improves every area of the company on a continual basis. Shows how the major improvement tools are applied in a matrix management model.
ISBN 0-915299-06-2 / 232 pages / $36.95

Productivity Press, Dept. BK, P.O. Box 3007, Cambridge, MA 02140 1-800-274-9911

BOOKS AVAILABLE FROM PRODUCTIVITY PRESS

Buehler, Vernon M. and Y.K. Shetty (eds.). **Competing Through Productivity and Quality**
ISBN 0-915299-43-7 / 1989 / 576 pages / $39.95 / order code COMP

Christopher, William F. **Productivity Measurement Handbook**
ISBN 0-915299-05-4 / 1985 / 680 pages / $137.95 / order code PMH

Ford, Henry. **Today and Tomorrow**
ISBN 0-915299-36-4 / 1988 / 286 pages / $24.95 / order code FORD

Fukuda, Ryuji. **Managerial Engineering: Techniques for Improving Quality and Productivity in the Workplace**
ISBN 0-915299-09-7 / 1984 / 206 pages / $34.95 / order code ME

Hatakeyama, Yoshio. **Manager Revolution! A Guide to Survival in Today's Changing Workplace**
ISBN 0-915299-10-0 / 1985 / 208 pages / $24.95 / order code MREV

Hirano, Hiroyuki. **JIT Factory Revolution: A Pictorial Guide to Factory Design of the Future**
ISBN 0-915299-44-5 / 1989 / 208 pages / $49.95 / order code JITFAC

Japan Human Relations Association (ed.). **The Idea Book: Improvement Through TEI (Total Employee Involvement)**
ISBN 0-915299-22-4 / 1988 / 232 pages / $49.95 / order code IDEA

Japan Management Association (ed.). **Kanban and Just-In-Time at Toyota: Management Begins at the Workplace** (Revised Ed.), *Translated by David J. Lu*
ISBN 0-915299-48-8 / 1989 / 192 pages / $34.95 / order code KAN

Japan Management Association and Constance E. Dyer. **The Canon Production System: Creative Involvement of the Total Workforce**
ISBN 0-915299-06-2 / 1987 / 251 pages / $36.95 / order code CAN

Karatsu, Hajime. **Tough Words For American Industry**
ISBN 0-915299-25-9 / 1988 / 178 pages / $24.95 / order code TOUGH

Karatsu, Hajime. **TQC Wisdom of Japan: Managing for Total Quality Control,** *Translated by David J. Lu*
ISBN 0-915299-18-6 / 1988 / 125 pages / $34.95 / order code WISD

Lu, David J. **Inside Corporate Japan: The Art of Fumble-Free Management**
ISBN 0-915299-16-X / 1987 / 278 pages / $24.95 / order code ICJ

Monden, Yashuhiro and Sakurai, Michiharu. **Japanese Management Accounting**
ISBN 0-915299-50-X / 1989 / 512 pages / $49.95 / order code JMACT

Mizuno, Shigeru (ed.). **Management for Quality Improvement: The 7 New QC Tools**
ISBN 0-915299-29-1 / 1988 / 304 pages / $59.95 / order code 7TQC

Nakajima, Seiichi. **Introduction to TPM: Total Productive Maintenance**
ISBN 0-915299-23-2 / 1988 / 129 pages / $39.95 / order code ITPM

Productivity Press, Inc., Dept. BK, P.O. Box 3007, Cambridge, MA 02140 1-800-274-9911

Nakajima, Seiichi. **TPM Development Program: Implementing Total Productive Maintenance**
ISBN 0-915299-37-2 / 1989 / 528 pages / $85.00 / order code DTPM

Nikkan Kogyo Shimbun, Ltd./Factory Magazine (ed.). **Poka-yoke: Improving Product Quality by Preventing Defects**
ISBN 0-915299-31-3 / 1989 / 288 pages / $59.95 / order code IPOKA

Ohno, Taiichi. **Toyota Production System: Beyond Large-Scale Production**
ISBN 0-915299-14-3 / 1988 / 162 pages / $39.95 / order code OTPS

Ohno, Taiichi. **Workplace Management**
ISBN 0-915299-19-4 / 1988 / 165 pages / $34.95 / order code WPM

Ohno, Taiichi and Setsuo Mito. **Just-In-Time for Today and Tomorrow: A Total Management System**
ISBN 0-915299-20-8 / 1988 / 208 pages / $34.95 / order code OMJIT

Psarouthakis, John. **Better Makes Us Best**
ISBN 0-915299-56-9 / 1989 / 112 pages / $16.95 / order code BMUB

Shingo, Shigeo. **Non-Stock Production: The Shingo System for Continuous Improvement**
ISBN 0-915299-30-5 / 1988 / 480 pages / $75.00 / order code NON

Shingo, Shigeo. **A Revolution In Manufacturing: The SMED System,** *Translated by Andrew P. Dillon*
ISBN 0-915299-03-8 / 1985 / 383 pages / $65.00 / order code SMED

Shingo, Shigeo. **The Sayings of Shigeo Shingo: Key Strategies for Plant Improvement,** *Translated by Andrew P. Dillon*
ISBN 0-915299-15-1 / 1987 / 207 pages / $36.95 / order code SAY

Shingo, Shigeo. **A Study of the Toyota Production System from an Industrial Engineering Viewpoint** (Revised Ed.)
ISBN 0-915299-17-8 / 1989 / 400 pages / $TBA / order code STREV

Shingo, Shigeo. **Zero Quality Control: Source Inspection and the Poka-yoke System,** *Translated by Andrew P. Dillon*
ISBN 0-915299-07-0 / 1986 / 328 pages / $65.00 / order code ZQC

Shinohara, Isao (ed.). **New Production System: JIT Crossing Industry Boundaries**
ISBN 0-915299-21-6 / 1988 / 224 pages / $34.95 / order code NPS

Sugiyama, Tomō. **The Improvement Book: Creating the Problem-free Workplace**
ISBN 0-915299-47-X / 1989 / 320 pages / $49.95 / order code IB-BK

Tateisi, Kazuma. **The Eternal Venture Spirit: An Executive's Practical Philosophy**
ISBN 0-915299-55-0 / 1989 / 208 pages / $19.95 / order code EVS

Productivity Press, Inc., Dept. BK, P.O. Box 3007, Cambridge, MA 02140 1-800-274-9911

AUDIO-VISUAL PROGRAMS

Japan Management Association. **Total Productive Maintenance: Maximizing Productivity and Quality**
ISBN 0-915299-46-1 / 167 slides / 1989 / $749.00 / order code STPM
ISBN 0-915299-49-6 / 2 videos / 1989 / $749.00 / order code VTPM

Shingo, Shigeo. **The SMED System,** *Translated by Andrew P. Dillon*
ISBN 0-915299-11-9 / 181 slides / 1986 / $749.00 / order code S5
ISBN 0-915299-27-5 / 2 videos / 1987 / $749.00 / order code V5

Shingo, Shigeo. **The Poka-yoke System,** *Translated by Andrew P. Dillon*
ISBN 0-915299-13-5 / 235 slides / 1987 / $749.00 / order code S6
ISBN 0-915299-28-3 / 2 videos / 1987 / $749.00 / order code V6

TO ORDER: Write, phone, or fax Productivity Press, Dept. BK, P.O. Box 3007, Cambridge, MA 02140, phone 1-800-274-9911, fax 617-868-3524. Send check or charge to your credit card (American Express, Visa, MasterCard accepted).

U.S. ORDERS: Add $4 shipping for first book, $2 each additional. CT residents add 7.5% and MA residents 5% sales tax.

FOREIGN ORDERS: Payment must be made in U.S. dollars (checks must be drawn on U.S. banks). For Canadian orders, add $10 shipping for first book, $2 each additional. For orders to other countries write, phone, or fax for quote and indicate shipping method desired.

NOTE: Prices subject to change without notice.